SECRETS OF A
MASTER CLOSER

A SIMPLER, EASIER, AND FASTER WAY TO SELL ANYTHING TO ANYONE, ANYTIME, ANYWHERE

MIKE KAPLAN

Cover Designed by: Damon Freeman

Typesetting by Kiersten Lief

Published by: Master Closers, Inc.

www.secretsofamastercloser.com

CONTENTS

INTRODUCTION
WHY READ THIS BOOK?

SELLING HAS BEEN DEFINED AS:

THE ACT OF PERSUADING OR CONVINCING SOMEONE TO BUY YOUR PRODUCT, SERVICE, OR IDEA.

Your ability to sell is determined by your ability to persuade or convince others.

Anyone who wants to maximize their ability to sell, or maximize the abilities of others to sell, should read this book.

This includes new salespeople, veteran salespeople, sales managers, sales trainers, negotiators, entrepreneurs and business owners.

The information in this book was compiled and refined over many years of my own personal sales experiences as well as my experiences in training thousands of others in sales. Not only have I sifted through numerous informational sources on my quest to discover the actual fundamentals of successful selling, everything in this book has also been extensively field-tested and proven to be successful. This is what I learned and used to become the #1 salesperson in my industry and to double my sales income every year for four straight years. I later found and built one of the fastest growing sales companies in the U.S. by training my sales staff on these same fundamentals.

When I first started in sales, I had no prior training, nor did I have any innate ability to persuade others. Instead, I relied on my ability to observe and emulate what other successful salespeople were doing. While this helped me to get started, I eventually realized that I had collected many tricks of the trade, and gimmicks without really knowing the underlying basics of selling. If I wanted to reach my full potential, I knew that I had to do something about my gap in knowledge.

I set out on a quest to discover the underlying fundamentals that would explain and properly align all the tricks, gimmicks and phrases that I had been memorizing and robotically reciting every day. I wanted to know why they worked. I wanted to understand sales in a more scientific fashion. I also wanted a road map that would lay out the exact path to making any sale, and I wanted to detail each step and its true purpose. I wanted to cause sales to occur and feel completely in control of my income. I wanted to be the best salesperson I could be.

As I moved along on my quest and discovered each new fundamental, or piece of the puzzle, I raised my "selling I.Q." After much research and experimentation, I finally had all of the pieces of the puzzle and saw how they fit together into one easy-to-understand whole.

From that moment on, all of the confusions and mysteries that I had regarding how to consistently and systematically close sales were gone. I knew that I had mapped out a step-by-step process that would allow me to sell more than ever before.

With these fundamentals discovered and understood, I could evaluate any new sales techniques and quickly determine if they were valid, why they would work (or not), and whether I should use them or not. I also found that I was able to invent my own new techniques and wordings as needed.

I think back on the lost time, heartache, and hard knocks that I could have avoided if someone had handed me a book like this when I first decided to give sales a shot. As it has been said, "It's water (or lost sales) under the bridge."

There are many great sales books, tapes, and systems available. Each one has something that will help you become a better salesperson. But, if you want to fully understand and maximize the benefits from those techniques and systems, *you need to know the underlying principles and fundamentals of selling*.

If you are new to sales, make this book the first one you read, and you will greatly increase your chances for early success. If you are a seasoned veteran and are looking for ways to improve your numbers (which all good salespeople always are), this book will help make your sales goals a reality. There is a very good chance that, while reading these pages, you'll find the clouds parting with a brighter understanding of selling shining through.

If you are a sales manager, trainer and/or business owner, make this book the cornerstone of your sales training. As my sales career advanced into sales management and eventually into owning my own sales company, I used the information in this book to build a sales training system that was the backbone of what became a multi-million dollar software sales company.

So, let's start your journey to record-shattering sales where I first started: the question of, "What *is* selling, really?"

1

WHAT IS SELLING?

SELLING IS A PROCESS. IT IS A PROCESS of persuading or convincing someone to buy your product, service, or idea.

A process is an "organized series of actions directed to some end." If someone understands and completely knows the process involved in any activity, then he or she can be successful in that activity. Without knowing the process of an activity you're involved in, you're destined for uncertainty, confusion and poor performance.

If you know the exact process of selling and can apply it correctly, you will succeed. That is a fact.

I was exposed to many techniques early on in my sales career. I followed them blindly without really knowing why they worked (when they did) or when and how to best use them. I figured that if other salespeople were using them, then I should too.

This served me pretty well when I first got started. I would watch and listen to the better salespeople in the company, and if I heard something that seemed to get them a good result, then I would use it. I also knew I couldn't rely only on a limited number of successful 'tricks' that I stole from other salespeople. I needed to have a deeper understanding.

I decided to invest a portion of my time in the evenings after work to study and learn sales techniques from the experts. I acquired one of the best lecture series on sales training that I have ever heard (currently titled "Back to the Future in Sales") by J. Douglas Edwards, considered the "Father of American Selling." I listened to these sales tapes over and over every evening and noted the techniques that made sense to me and that I felt I could put to use in my sales. Onto small cards, I wrote down wordings that were appropriate for my product and industry.

The next day at work, I placed these cards in front of me so that I could see them when making my sales calls. I would test the technique at the appropriate time during a sales call and note the result. I gave each technique three tries to see if it would work. If it did, I kept it and made it part of my own bag of tricks. If it didn't, I tossed it.

I continued to do this for several months with each of J. Douglas Edward's lectures, and later I did the same with all other sales lectures or books I could get my hands on. As a result, I built up a great arsenal of field-tested sales techniques that I knew worked for me.

Although I had learned many new techniques and my sales had increased, I still felt like something wasn't right. I had dozens of memorized techniques floating in my head that I could draw from, but I knew something fundamental was missing that was keeping me from reaching my full potential as a salesman.

I had wondered if there was an underlying system of fundamental laws that applied to every sale that would make sense of and properly align all of my memorized techniques. Was there a basic anatomy of selling that could be applied universally to every sale? Was there a common series of steps or a uniform process that applied to all successful sales transactions?

I decided to reverse engineer (taking something apart and analyzing its workings in detail) a sale by starting from the end and working backwards to the beginning to make sure I had every step of the process.

I simply started off by asking, "What is the very final step of a sale?" That was easy, and I noted down the obvious: The final step was when the prospect (potential buyer) owned the product or service. With that answer, I then asked, "What has to happen right before a buyer 'owns it' to make that happen?" And once that was answered, I asked again, "What has to happen right before that to make that happen?" and so on, all the way back to the first step that starts the sale process.

It may sound too simple, but by doing this, I uncovered vital steps in my sales process that were missing! These missing steps turned out to be the difference in being an average salesperson and being the very best.

With all the steps discovered I now had a 'Road Map' to follow for any sale.

THE 8-STEP ROAD MAP TO UNLIMITED SALES

Prospect owns product

↑

8. Buys product   Close

↑

7. Wants product

↑

6. Aware of product and how it solves his/her problem

↑

5. Attention directed to product features/benefits   Presentation

↑

4. Wants problem solved and wants to hear solution

↑

3. Problem found

↑

2. Qualified

↑

1. Introduction   Pre-Presentation

See how this works?

Before someone will **own** a product, he (of course) has to **buy** it. Before he will buy it, he has to **want** it. Before he will want it, he has to be **aware** of how it will solve his problem. To do that, the prospect has to have his **attention directed** to the **features** and **benefits** of the product that will solve his problem, and he won't let that happen unless he first **wants his problem solved**—and that won't happen until his **problem is found**.

These steps also fit into three general stages of a sale:

Pre-Presentation → Presentation → Close

When all these steps were uncovered, I truly knew for the first time what the process of selling was all about, and once I learned how to accomplish each of these steps my confidence and closing percentages soared. I understood exactly where I was headed when I started every sale. I knew at all times where I was in the process and exactly how to get to the close.

If any of these steps is missing, you're going to have a hard time making sales because each one is a fundamental building block to build a completed sale (a close). Each block is built upon the previous block. Each step is done to be able to accomplish the next step. If a step is skipped or poorly performed it can negatively affect the outcome of the sale.

For instance, a salesperson is going to have little chance of closing a sale if she jumps right into her presentation, telling the prospect all about her product's features without having first discovered which problems are important to the prospect. Also, the salesperson will have trouble if she fails to get the prospect's willingness to want to solve his problem and to listen to a presentation. A salesperson will also have trouble closing the prospect on the price of his product or service unless the prospect is first closed on wanting the product or service. Not knowing how to achieve each step or to recognize when a step has been accomplished and move to the next in a timely manner will also cause failures.

The following chapters will fully explain each step of the 8-Step Road Map, from the bottom up, including its purpose, how to achieve it, and sample scripted wordings.

Once you fully understand each step and its purpose, you will be able to work out your own precise wordings that fit your business, product or service, and can test them in the field.

While the 8-Step Road Map works as I have laid it out for most industries, products, and services, there may be circumstances peculiar to your sales that require some adjustments. I suggest that you do what I did many years ago and make any needed modifications by reverse engineering and working out your ideal process by starting from the final step and traveling backwards step by step to uncover any parts unique to your company or product.

At the end of each chapter there is a series of exercises that will assist you in mastering the principles you just learned. I strongly recommend that you do not skip these exercises if you want to become the best salesperson possible.

EXERCISES:

Write your answers on a separate piece of paper.

1. What is selling?

   CONVINCE TO BUY OUR PRODUCT

2. Reverse engineer your own sales process for your particular product or service to see if it is different than the 8-Step process identified in this chapter. Start by asking, "What is the final step of the sale?" Write that down. Then ask, "What has to happen just before <u>that</u> for the final step to happen?" Write that down below your first answer. Repeat until you have traced every step back to the introduction step. When you ask these questions, put yourself in the position of the prospect and think about what has to happen with him on that step.

3. Type or neatly write out your road map steps and place them somewhere on your desk where they can be easily seen.

4. What are the three general stages of a sale?

   - *PRE- PRESENTATION*
   - *PRESENTATION*
   - *CLOSE*

5. Give two examples of a step that could be missing from the sales process and describe what could occur as a result. *Sument to Produu*

   PRICE

6. What should you know about each step of the 8-Step Road Map before working out a wording or script for that step?

2

THREE TYPES OF SALESPEOPLE

THERE ARE THREE TYPES OF SALESPEOPLE:

- Order Takers
- Presenters
- Closers

THESE THREE TYPES OF SALESPEOPLE ARE DETERMINED BY THEIR ABILITY TO CONTROL OR DIRECT THEIR PROSPECTS AND PERSUADE OR CONVINCE THEM TO BUY.

Before reading further, take a second to look at a clock or your watch and note the time. Go ahead, do this now and then continue reading.

Just like you can control or direct your own body or control the driving of a car, you can also control or direct another person's attention. If you had looked at the time when I asked, I was then able to control or direct your attention to a clock. As a result, I made you aware of the time. A salesperson does the same thing when he controls and directs a prospect's attention to the various features of his product or service and makes her aware of how it will solve her problem. He does this on a step-by-step basis, directing the prospect through each step of the 8-Step Road Map until the prospect desires and wants the product or service.

THE MORE ABLE AND WILLING YOU ARE TO CON-TROL OR DIRECT YOUR PROSPECT IN A POSITIVE MANNER THROUGH THE STEPS OF THE ROAD MAP, THE MORE SALES AND MONEY YOU WILL EARN.

Let's examine the three types of salespeople and the differences in the amount of control or direction used by each.

Order Takers, as the name suggests, only take orders (requests for purchases). Their job is to process an order that a prospect originates.

Order Takers are typically not involved in persuading or convincing someone to buy something. They may answer questions and point out various choices regarding their product line or services, if asked, but Order Takers do not proactively cause a sale to occur. The prospect, typically induced by advertising or other means, has decided on her own to make the purchase. The Order Taker exercises very little to no control or direction of the prospect on any step of the sale.

Examples of Order Takers include counter clerks in department stores and telephone operators who take calls from prospects who want to buy a product they saw in a TV infomercial or in a catalogue. Order Takers are very useful and important to a business, particularly businesses that use effective marketing and advertising that does all of the work to persuade or convince someone to buy.

Presenters, again as the name suggests, specialize in presenting their product or service to prospects. They typically use their presentation (the giving of information) to inform and enlighten prospects about the features of their products or services. They can control or direct the prospect's attention to the features of their product or service, but lack control and direction of the prospect on the other vital steps of the 8-Step Road Map.

At their best, Presenters are confident, know every detail about their product or service, and can answer any question asked by a prospect. They can be very articulate, knowledgeable, methodical, and thorough. They can also be very caring and sincerely interested. Presenters, however, rely solely on their presentation (and product knowledge) in hopes that it will create enough interest in what they are selling for a prospect to buy.

Presenters include those who work trade shows presenting to several prospects at the same time, and salespeople on the home shopping TV channels. Like Order Takers, they provide a valuable service for many businesses.

A Closer, as the name implies, specializes in closing (or completing) sales.

A CLOSER KNOWS HOW TO CONTROL AND DIRECT THE PROSPECT'S ATTENTION THROUGHOUT EACH STEP OF THE SALE AND IS WILLING TO DO SO.

Closers are in full control of each step. They are 100% involved and leave nothing to chance. They are highly skilled in persuading or convincing someone to buy their products, services, or ideas. They have all the skills of the best presenter and much, much more. They don't rely solely on presentations to make sales, but use them as one of their many tools.

Closers know the precise steps required to get someone to buy and have the know-how, certainty and confidence to get each step fully done. They know where the sale is going at all times and follow the 8-Step Road Map to the close. They do not hope for sales to occur, but actively cause them.

A scale for the three types of salespeople according to their ability to cause or determine sales at will looks like this:

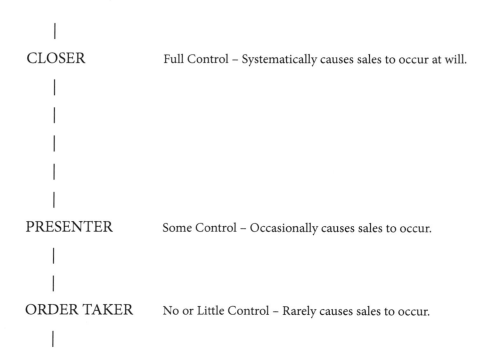

CLOSER   Full Control – Systematically causes sales to occur at will.

PRESENTER   Some Control – Occasionally causes sales to occur.

ORDER TAKER   No or Little Control – Rarely causes sales to occur.

Order Takers are at the bottom of the scale as they do little or nothing to CAUSE a sale to happen. They are, in actuality, the EFFECT of a sale occurring. Presenters are a bit higher up on the scale as they are causing the presentation, which they hope will bring the prospect up to interest resulting in a sale.

CLOSERS, AT THE TOP OF THE SCALE, CAUSE EACH RE-QUIRED STEP THAT LEADS TO A SALE OCCURRING.

They use various tools and techniques to bring this about. They leave nothing to chance and don't just hope for sales to close, they CAUSE them.

By understanding and following a road map that details every step needed to close a sale, Closers know exactly where to go and how to get there.

Using the analogy of flying an airplane, Presenters may know how to get the airplane to take off but, once airborne, they don't know their final destination and, even if they did, don't know the shortest guaranteed route to get there before running out of fuel.

Closers, on the other hand, can take off, know exactly where they are flying at all times, can read the navigation instruments, get through any turbulence (prospect objections), stay on course, and make safe landings.

Presenter: Closer:

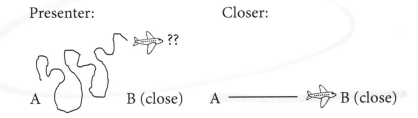

Closers know how to take a sale from point A to point B. They not only know that a straight path exists, but also know how to get on that path and stay on it all the way to the close. They are always directing and steering the sale from A to B as a fast as possible, knowing that the faster they do so, the more sales they make in the time they have, and the more money they earn.

What made Michael Jordan the greatest basketball player who ever lived, and what put him above all the other talented players? To start, his obvious ability to score more points than anyone else. We know MJ was a great shooter but, in order for a great shooter to score points he must have opportunities to shoot the ball. What separated MJ from all others was his ability to create or *cause* opportunities to shoot when none existed! He didn't wait or hope for opportunities to present themselves. He proactively caused them. Where a split second earlier there was no open lane or open shot, MJ could make one appear (perhaps with a head fake or spin). Once he created the opportunity, he didn't hesitate or let it slip by. He caused the opportunities and *acted* on them—just like a Closer does with sales.

Closers, like Michael Jordan, focus their efforts on three things:

KNOWING *HOW TO CREATE OPPORTUNITIES* TO CLOSE → KNOWING *WHEN* TO CLOSE → KNOWING *HOW* TO CLOSE

A person can be successful being an Order Taker or Presenter if that's what the sales position calls for. If it calls for anything more, then a salesperson needs to be the best Closer they can be. Every salesperson ranks somewhere on the above scale. As you learn more, you will move higher up on this scale. The higher you are on this scale, the more sales you can cause to occur.

The rest of this book is dedicated to helping you reach the highest point on this scale possible.

EXERCISES:

Write your answers on a separate piece of paper.

1. What are the three types of salespeople?

2. What is the single most important factor that defines these three types of salespeople?

3. Describe the differences between the three types of sales people.

4. What are the three things a Closer focuses her efforts on?

3

THE INTRODUCTION

MOST EVERY SALE, AFTER THE FIRST contact has been made with a prospect, starts with some sort of introduction. The introduction step will vary according to the circumstances (for example, cold calling a prospect who is not expecting your call versus a prospect that has called you), but the purpose is essentially the same.

THE PURPOSE OF THE FIRST STEP, INTRODUCTION, IS TO GRAB THE PROSPECT'S ATTENTION AND ESTABLISH CONTROL OF THE CONVERSATION.

This is done by:

1) Briefly telling the prospect who you are and the reason for your call or conversation.

2) Getting the prospect's agreement to be asked some questions and willingness to listen to what you have to say.

And, at the same time…

3) Telling the prospect you want to determine if you can be of any help or service to him or her.

1. BRIEFLY TELL THE PROSPECT WHO YOU ARE AND THE REASON WHY YOU ARE CALLING:

Example:

"Hi _____, this is Mike Kaplan, I'm with XYZ Company. How are you today? Great, the reason for my call is_____."

or,

"Hi _____, this is Mike Kaplan, I'm with XYZ Company. How are you today? Great, let me tell you why I'm calling. I..."

Always start with who you are and the company you're with as a matter of good etiquette. It will also orient the prospect to who is calling.

The reason for your call must grab their attention. Ideally, it will be something that will encourage your prospects to stop whatever they're doing and want to listen to what you have to say.

It could be the biggest benefit of your product or service, or simply what you do, or want to do for the prospect. It could be that you're responding to their earlier request to be contacted or sent more information.

Keep it simple and to as few words as possible. If it is too long winded, your prospects are unlikely to get it, and you won't grab their attention. You are not trying to close them on your product or service with the introduction; you are only trying to grab their attention.

If you're cold calling or otherwise originating the contact, you're most likely interrupting something the prospects were in the middle of. They don't know why you're calling, and you will have very little time to grab their attention before they possibly get annoyed.

Finding the best reason for your call to use in your introduction might require some testing. Come up with several reasons, and try them out on several calls. The best will register quickly and grab the majority of the prospects' attention.

When I was selling, I tested a few different reasons for calling until I found the one that was concise and most consistently obtained the best results and then I stuck with it for years. You can do the same.

Example:

Years ago, I sold sales leads (prospect names) to sales firms. I started with this reason for calling and used it for a period of time:

"...the reason for my call is we provide fresh sales leads to firms like yours that could boost your sales closing percentage..."

I later found that most every firm I called was always looking for another lead source, and I had their attention as soon as I said,

"...we provide fresh sales leads for firms like yours..."

So I shortened it and used it from that point on without any need to change it up. The point is to create some of your own introductions based on your product or service and test them.

Another example:

I owned a sales company that sold products to PC and network technicians so they could diagnose and repair computer systems.

"...the reason for my call is we provide tools that help technicians cut down the time it takes to diagnose and repair PCs and networks..."

More examples:

Continuing education courses:

"...the reason for my call is we provide the fastest and least expensive way for accountants to fulfill their continuing education requirement..."

Gas and electric utilities:

"...we have a program that can cut your power bill down by as much as 30%..."

You get the idea? Try several to find the one that gets you the best response (a real attention grabber), and stick with it.

2. GET THE PROSPECT'S AGREEMENT TO BE ASKED SOME QUESTIONS AND HIS WILLINGNESS TO LISTEN TO WHAT YOU HAVE TO SAY.

You just told the prospect your name, the company that you're with and the reason for your call. The next step is to get his agreement that you can ask some questions and also briefly explain what you have to offer.

You need this agreement to establish control of the conversation and move to the next step on the 8-Step Road Map, Qualify, where you will be asking specific questions to determine if the prospect could and should buy your product or service.

With his agreement given, the prospect is, in essence, agreeing to allow you to direct the conversation through the asking of questions. Whoever is asking the questions is in control and is directing the attention of the other person.

Examples:

"...I'd like to take a second and ask you a few questions then tell you briefly what we have, would that be ok?"

or,

"...I'd like to ask you a few questions to see if what we have is appropriate to your needs and then tell you briefly what it is about, would that be ok?"

When you get a "yes" to this, you have your first small agreement and have permission to take control of the conversation and start directing the prospect's attention.

SELLING (THE ACT OF PERSUADING) IS A PROCESS MADE UP OF GETTING SEVERAL SMALL AGREEMENTS OR CLOSES, LEADING TO THE MAJOR (and final) AGREEMENT OR CLOSE (where the prospect agrees to the purchase and payment).

The purpose of the introduction is not to close prospects on buying, but only to close them on allowing you to ask some questions and briefly explain what you have to offer.

3. TELL THE PROSPECT YOU WANT TO DETERMINE IF YOU CAN BE OF ANY HELP OR SERVICE TO HIM.

Why do this?

Let me ask you—Would you be willing to invest your time as a prospect and get involved in a sales presentation if you didn't feel like the salesperson was there to help you?

Would you let the salesperson start to control your attention by asking you questions and/or telling you about her product if you didn't feel like she was trying to help? Worse, what would you do if you sensed that the salesperson was only there to make a buck?

Most prospects will be resistive to you taking control and trying to sell them if they don't feel like you are there to help them, or if they sense that your only motivation is making money.

Prospects might already assume that you are there to help when you tell them the reason for your call but let's not take that chance. As part of your introduction, tell them and make them really understand that you want to see if you can be of any help or service to them.

By the way, isn't that what selling is all about—providing products or services that help people? The more you can do that, the more you will love what you do, and the more money you will make.

THE FULL INTRODUCTION STEP

"Hi _____, this is Mike Kaplan, I'm with XYZ Company. How are you today? Great, the reason for my call is_____, and I'd like to take a second and ask you a few questions to see if I could possibly be of any help, then tell you briefly what we have, would that be ok?"

In this very simple wording, the purpose of the introduction is achieved. This is only one example but it's a great one that has served me very well for years. You may have to modify it for your business, product, or service. Just make sure that the purpose (closing them on allowing you to ask questions) is achieved.

Do not pause or hesitate while saying your introduction, particularly after you give the reason. Except for waiting for the prospect's answer to "How are you doing today?" the introduction should be said all in one breath and sound like one sentence. You want to get that "yes."

MORE ON YOUR ABILITY TO CONTROL THE SALE

AN IMPORTANT FACTOR IN YOUR SUCCESS IN SELLING REQUIRES THAT YOU HAVE THE WILLINGNESS AND SKILL TO TAKE CONTROL OF (TO DIRECT IN A POSITIVE MANNER) THE PROSPECT'S ATTENTION.

You will see as we progress through the 8-Step Road Map that you, as a Closer, will be directing the prospect's attention throughout the entire sales process.

On the Introduction step, you want to establish this control in a smooth, efficient and professional manner. Steps 1-3 above will achieve this.

The amount of effort it will take to establish this control is determined by who made the initial contact. Is the prospect calling you and reaching out to you by responding to an advertisement? If so, it should be relatively easy to establish control. In this case, Step #1 wouldn't include the reason for your call, but would include asking for the prospect's full name and phone number.

If the prospect approached you by sending a request (via the web or mail) for more information about your product or service and you are calling them back for the first time, it might take a little more effort to grab their attention and establish control.

Cold calling typically requires the most effort and skill to grab a prospect's attention and establish control. In this case, your introduction must be crisp and to the point as you have essentially interrupted whatever the prospect was doing and may only have a short window to capture his attention. Unless the prospect has called you, he isn't waiting in his office or home hoping for salespeople to call.

Some prospects, when you are cold calling or calling leads that are very old, instantly put their guard up if they sense that you are a salesperson. They may get resistive, even hostile, once you tell them the reason for your call. In these cases, an alternative reason for calling and another approach may be needed that is less direct yet ultimately achieves the same purpose.

Example:

"Hi _____, this is Mike Kaplan, I'm with XYZ Company. How are you today? Great, the reason for my call is we're conducting a marketing survey regarding (<u>*something related to your product or service*</u>*) and I was wondering if you wouldn't mind me asking you a few questions, as part of the survey. Would that be ok?"*

or,

"...conducting a marketing survey of experts regarding (<u>*something related to your product or service*</u>*)..."*

Many prospects who might have been resistive to other introductions will be willing to answer questions for a survey. The survey questions used should accomplish the next two steps of the 8-Step Road Map (Qualify and Find the Problem) and, if done correctly, will allow the Closer to smoothly transition into the Presentation.

MORE EXAMPLES

You can get as creative as you want as long as you achieve the purpose of grabbing the prospect's attention and establishing control of the conversation.

Closer: "Hi _____, this is Mike Kaplan, I'm with XYZ Company. If someone called you out of the blue and told you they had a guaranteed way to_____, would you give them 5 minutes to let them tell you about it?"

Prospect: "Yes."

Closer: "Great! Can I first take a second and ask you a few questions to see how I can best be of help?"

Here is a sample wording if the prospect has called you in response to an advertisement:

Prospect: "I saw your website and wanted to know more about your product."

Closer: "That's great! I can help you with that. My name is Mike. Can I get your name?"

Prospect: "Joe."

Closer: "And what number are you calling from, Joe?"

Prospect: "555-555-5555."

Closer: "Joe, would it be okay to ask you a couple of questions to see how I can best help you and then tell you what we have?"

Prospect: "Yes."

If you offer something free, like a newsletter, it can help in getting the contact information, building rapport, and establishing control.

"Okay, I can certainly help you with that. First, I wanted to let you

know we have a newsletter that we send out to all of our clients that's free of charge. If you give me your name and address, I can get that out to you. I think you'll find it very informative."

If the prospect sent a request for more information (via the mail or internet):

"This is Mike Kaplan with XYZ Company, the reason for my call is that you recently requested information on _____, and I wanted to ask you a few questions to see how I could be of service and then tell you what it's all about, would that be ok?"

Please note that, whatever the introduction, your communication needs to be precise, clear, and positive and you must come across as being very interested in the prospect. This is no place to be fumbling around and figuring out what to say as you go.

Test various wordings and determine the best introduction for your particular product or service and business. Create variations for cold calling on a prospect (if that's what you do), a prospect calling you, and returning a prospect's call. Then practice them until your delivery is smooth and confident.

CALL-BACK INTRODUCTIONS

A call-back is a call placed or a visit made to the prospect as a follow up to an initial call or visit. The introduction for call-backs is somewhat different and is dependent upon what happened by the end of the first or previous call (or visit). Introductions for call-backs are discussed later in chapter 13, after you have become familiar with the other steps of the 8-Step Road Map.

BRUSH OFFS

If a prospect says that he's not interested or too busy and is trying to brush you off, you can rephrase your reason for calling to make it more compelling:

Closer: "I do realize that you're busy, but if I had something that could solve your _____ and at the same time could _____, wouldn't it be a big benefit to you to know what it is?"

Prospect: "Yes."

Closer: "Okay, so let's invest 5 minutes to find out what it is, and if after that you don't see any value, then we'll move on, fair enough?"

or,

"I know you're busy, but we're talking about an opportunity to _____ that will_____. Come on, invest 5 minutes and see if this is for you. If after that you don't see any value, then we'll move on, okay?"

If it <u>really</u> isn't a good time:

"Ok, no problem. When is a better time to call back later today: early afternoon or later in the day?" Pin down a time that the prospect agrees to.

If the prospect becomes upset or angry as a result of your introduction (which can occasionally happen), you can calm him down by saying:

"I'm not trying to sell you anything today, I just want to ask you a few questions to see if I can be of any service and get you some information, would that be ok?"

An easy brush-off for the prospect to use early on in a first call is for him to ask:

"Do you have any information you can send me?"

You can answer:

"Yes, and that's why I need to ask a few questions—to determine exactly what I should send that will best help you, ok? Let me ask you..."

If you cannot get past the request to "just send information," there is still a way to get all the answers you'll need:

> Prospect: *"Do you have something (or information) you can send me?"*

> Closer: *"Sure, I'll need your mailing address."*

In between parts of the address, you ask your questions (see the next two chapters). The prospect will relax because he thinks the call is about to end and won't mind answering "just one more question."

"Just one last thing before I let you go..."

In many cases, the prospect will be drawn back into your call and may forget he had "no time right now," and you can keep the sale moving to the next step.

Another common brush-off is when the prospect asks very early on, *"How much does it cost?"*

It is a good sign to hear this later, well into the presentation, but when prospects asks this during the introduction, or shortly after, they are often attempting to use the price as a reason not to go any further. Imagine a balancing scale that has two trays. One tray is for the price; the other is for all the benefits (value) of your product or service. If you give the price without giving the benefits that are important to the prospect, the scale will tip to one side, the price. How can prospects justify the price without really knowing how the product or service will benefit them and solve their problems or needs?

The Closer does her best to delay giving the price when asked early on:

> *"The price depends on exactly what your order will be and that depends on what you'll need. That's why I want to simply ask you a few questions and briefly tell you about the (product/service) and then be able to work up a price, fair enough?"*

or,

> *"Well, it depends on what model you order and the features you*

get, which I will go over and then we can get into the cost, ok?"

If the prospect insists on knowing the price, then give a range that is realistic, saying something like this:

"The price ranges from $_____ to $_____. But your actual price will depend on exactly what you order, and that depends on what will best suit you. Plus, we have various discounts and specials that will make the price even more attractive. But let's forget about the price for a second, because it is meaningless until you can see the value. Give me a few minutes to ask a few questions, and then I'll tell you what it is about, fair enough?"

If the prospect still tries to brush you off after you gave him the price, you can try (in a friendly tone):

"Now, be fair. I told you the price without any opportunity to first show you how you would benefit from my product/service. At least give me 5 minutes and a chance to prove to you that my product/ service more than justifies the price. If, after 5 minutes, I fail to do that, then I'll let you go, fair enough?"

RECEPTIONISTS

To get to a prospect, a Closer will often have to go through a receptionist or assistant, particularly when selling a business-related product or service.

It is best, if possible, to make the receptionist or assistant your ally as they often decide who gets to talk to the prospect. They may come in handy down the road and can give you insight regarding their boss or the best times to reach him. They'll generally be more inclined to help you.

It's usually helpful to ask for the receptionist's or assistant's first name and from that point on to use it whenever you call the office. If they are not too busy, you can even make some small talk. They appreciate the simple recognition and will be more inclined to help you make contact with their boss.

"What's your name? (Betty.) Betty, my name is _____. I just got a note that he needed some information, and I'm just trying to get back to him."

or,

"All I have here is a note to call him, so I'm trying to get back to him."

In response to an e-mail or internet lead:

"I just got an e-mail from him. It looks like he wanted me to call him today."

Try as you may, some receptionists never quite warm up and will never be an ally to your cause. Some are mandated by their bosses to take messages only. They often say, *"He's on another line and asked me to take a message."* If this happens several times and you see very little hope of ever getting through, you need to get a bit more clever or forceful, or both.

Receptionist: "He's on another line and asked me to take a message."

Closer: "That's fine. I'll hold on."

Moments later...

Receptionist: "He's still on the line. Do you want to continue holding?"

Closer: "Yes, I'll hold."

Moments later...

Receptionist: "He's still on the line. Do you want me to take a message?"

Closer: "No, I'll hold on."

Moments later...

Receptionist: "He's off now. I'll put you through."

If the receptionist cannot get you to the prospect, then you'll have to either leave a message or let the receptionist know that you will try again later.

LEAVING MESSAGES

What about voice-mail? It can be a barrier as it makes it easy for a prospect to ignore your calls.

When you have not yet made initial contact with a prospect and you reach voice mail, you have to decide whether or not to leave a message. Use your own judgment, but sometimes it's best to not leave any message and to try calling again later to see if the prospect will pick up. If that doesn't work after a couple of times, you will need to leave a message.

Sometimes a simple message of just your name, number, and a request to call is all that is needed.

"Hi, this is Mike Kaplan. When you get a chance, please call me at…."

Many times, that type of message will be ignored, and you will want to leave a bit more.

"Hello _____, my name is Mike Kaplan. I'm calling about _____. When you get a chance, please call me at…"

Fill in what you're calling about with something general that relates to what you do but leaves the prospect wondering what it is, and wanting to call you back. In this approach, avoid mentioning that you are providing or selling something.

Examples:

Insurance: "I'm calling about your insurance premium payment."

Long distance service: "I'm calling about your phone bill."

Web design service: "I'm calling about something on your website."

Advertising: "I'm calling about your advertisement in ABC magazine."

Whatever type of message you leave, the goal is to inspire the prospect to call you back. Do not give your sales presentation in a voicemail message as that is not going to close a sale. You are only trying to *close the prospect on calling you back.*

Think about what you would want to hear in a message that would make you want to call someone back and come up with a few different messages to test. Keep track and use the message that gets you the best results.

You can also modify any of these examples and use them when leaving a message with a receptionist. Again, create your own and test them.

If a prospect wrote in (via direct mail or internet) asking for more information:

"This is Mike Kaplan. I have that information you requested. Please call me at_____, and I'll be able to go over it with you."

or,

"This is Mike Kaplan.   You wanted information on how to _____, and I just need to confirm your mailing address. Please call me at..."

Fill in the *"how to ____"* with the biggest problem you know that your product or service solves.

or,

"Hello _____, my name is Mike Kaplan. We've never met, but I was given your name. If you could call me back, I have some information I think you should know about (or, would benefit from). I'll be at the following number for a couple more hours..."

Be creative, but never leave a message that will irritate or upset the prospect. You should never leave a hostile, angry, or threatening message with any prospect or customer. Be professional at all times. Don't lie or be dishonest. While it may get prospects to call, they will be very upset to learn it was a pretense, and if they don't hang up, they will be more difficult to sell.

The introduction step establishes a foothold. This is where you make your first small sale, which is the prospect allowing you to ask questions and tell him what you have to offer. With his agreement you can now control the rest of the sale. A good introduction is one that makes the prospect want to hear what you have to say and one where you have earned the right to continue and control the conversation.

EXERCISES:

Write your answers on a separate piece of paper.

1. What is the purpose of the Introduction step?

2. What are the three steps to use to accomplish the purpose of the Introduction?

3. Write down two or three of the very best reasons for calling that you can use to grab your prospects' interest.

4. What is the reason for getting prospects' agreement to ask them some questions and then tell them briefly what you have to offer?

5. Selling is the process made up of getting what?

6. What is the purpose of telling prospects that you want to see if you can be of any help or service to them?

7. Write out your full Introduction for a first time contact of a prospect who hasn't called you first. Make sure all three parts are included. Then do the same for a prospect who has called you first.

8. Why is your willingness and skill to take control of (to direct in a positive manner) the prospect's attention an important factor in your success in selling?

9. Get with a friend or co-worker and practice saying your scripted introduction until you can say it without pausing or hesitating at any point. It should be said all in one breath and should sound like one sentence. Practice this until you can do it smoothly and confidently.

IMPORTANT: MOST OF THESE EXERCISES ARE DESIGNED TO TEACH YOU ONE SKILL AT A TIME, SO ONLY PRACTICE WHAT IS STATED IN THE EXERCISE.

TO GET THE MOST OUT OF THESE PRACTICE EXERCISES, IT IS BEST TO SPEND YOUR TIME ACTUALLY DOING THEM AND NOT JUST DISCUSSING THEM. THE MORE YOU PUT INTO ACTUAL PRACTICE, THE FASTER YOU WILL BECOME A MASTER CLOSER!

10. Practice with a friend or co-worker handling brush-offs. Practice this using multiple rejections until you can do it smoothly and confidently.

11. Practice with a friend or co-worker getting the receptionist to get you through to the prospect. Practice this until you can do it smoothly and confidently.

12. Practice with a friend or co-worker leaving the various types of messages. Practice this until you can do it smoothly and confidently.

Now that you have established control and have permission to ask questions, it's time to move to Step 2 on the 8-Step Road Map: Qualify.

4

QUALIFY

BEFORE SPENDING TOO MUCH TIME WITH a new prospect, you want to find out if she is a true potential buyer. You want to determine if your prospect is "qualified" to buy your product or service.

From a Closer's point of a view, a "qualified prospect" is one that you have determined can:

1) USE THE PRODUCT.

2) AUTHORIZE THE PURCHASE (OR GET IT AUTHO-RIZED).

3) PAY FOR IT.

You can try to do all of the other steps of this 8-Step Road Map expertly and still never close the sale if the prospect can't use or pay for your product or service.

As a salesperson, specifically as a Closer, you are making an investment of your time, energy, and skill each time you start to sell a new prospect. Therefore, you want to know as soon as possible if a person is a real prospect by finding out if she can use your product, authorize its purchase, and pay for it. If she cannot use it or pay for it, move on to the next prospect.

I need to mention that any lack of the prospect's <u>interest</u> in your product or service at this stage has nothing to do with whether the prospect is qualified. You can't really expect her to be interested since you haven't gone beyond Step 1, the Introduction.

IT IS THE CLOSER'S JOB TO BUILD THE PROSPECT'S IN-TEREST BY FOLLOWING ALL THE STEPS OF THE 8-STEP ROAD MAP.

The Qualification step can be quick. You actually want to spend as little time on it as you can.

How do you determine for yourself if a prospect is truly qualified?

In the previous step (Introduction), you got permission to ask the prospect questions. You will be using questions throughout the sales process as you follow the 8-Step Road Map. Some of those questions will be used to determine if your prospect is qualified to buy.

There are no set questions that you must ask as long as they are aimed at determining whether the prospect 1) can use 2) can authorize purchase of (or get authorization), and 3) can pay for your product or service.

Here are sample questions to determine if your prospect can <u>use</u> your product:

"What does your company do?"

"What are you currently using (or have) that _____?"

"What else are you using (or have) that _____?"

"What do you normally use to solve _____?"

"Can I assume that you keep your eyes open for new opportunities that might help _____?"

With these questions, you are trying to get enough information to determine if the prospect can use (and needs) your product. You might also uncover competitive solutions she's currently using or thinking of getting, which you may have to convince her (in your presentation) are not as good as yours.

Asking the prospect directly if she can use your product or service may not work because she knows nothing about it at this point. You can't expect her to know, but it is expected that <u>you</u> find this out. Simply ask questions and the answers will allow you to determine if the prospect can use (not necessarily wants) your product or service. These questions may be different depending on whether you are selling to an individual consumer, business owner, corporation, and so on.

In addition to the sample questions above, you should come up with any additional questions that would help you determine if your prospect could use (or needs) your particular product or service.

Note: After you ask any question of your prospects, be silent and allow them to answer. Don't interrupt the prospect's answer. Be prepared to ask the question again if the prospect doesn't answer directly.

Here are some sample questions you can ask to determine if the prospect has the <u>money</u> needed to make the purchase:

"What is your typical budget for _____?"

"Do you normally have money set aside for_____?"

"After I tell you about the opportunity I have, and if you like it, would between $_____ and $_____ be available (or in your budget)?"

"After I tell you about the opportunity I have, and if you decide it would be beneficial to your organization, would between $_____ and $_____ be available or in the budget?"

For an individual buying for personal use:

"What do you do for a living?"

Based on the prospect's answer, you may be able to estimate her ability to pay.

Here are some questions you can ask to determine if your prospect is the <u>decision maker</u> (can authorize the purchase):

"By the way, what is your position with the company?"

"Who's normally in charge of purchasing _____ for your company (your family)?"

"Other than yourself, is there anyone else involved in making these kinds of purchasing decisions?"

If there is someone else who needs to authorize the purchase:

"How does the approval process normally work?"

or,

"How does a final decision usually get made?"

These questions have been proven to work, but you can always come up with additional questions of your own and test them.

There are ways to determine if your prospect can use and pay for your product or service even before calling or making contact.

For instance, in my sales lead business, if I saw that a prospect was already advertising in several other magazines and/or using direct mail to generate sales prospects for her business, I already knew there was a good chance that 1) she can use my service, and 2) she can pay for it. Other than wanting to know the number of salespeople she had (the more the better), I only needed to determine if the prospect had the authority to make the purchase.

When selling high-end consumer products or investments, you can sometimes determine your prospects' ability to purchase simply by knowing what they do for a living, the neighborhood they live in, the house they own, or the car they drive.

However you handle the Qualify step, make it sound conversational. Avoid asking all of your questions one after the other, which makes it sound like an interrogation.

In my own experience, I would often mix qualifying questions with those from the next step of the 8-Step Road Map, Find the Problem (next chapter). For on that step, you'll be locating the problems, needs, and desires of the prospect, and it is easy to slip in a qualifying question or two. I found it sounded more natural and wasn't ever awkward for me or the prospect.

Use your own judgment, but remember, even though this step is listed as number two, you can ask qualifying questions at any time during the sales process. Of course, the earlier you get the answers, the earlier you'll know if you have a qualified prospect, which will keep you from wasting time.

If you understand the purpose of the Qualify step and the three things you need to know, you can create your own questions or ways to accomplish this step.

As soon as you have determined that the prospect is qualified, move onto Step 3 of the 8-Step Road Map. If you determined he or she is not qualified, move on to the next prospect.

EXERCISES:

Write your answers on a separate piece of paper.

1. What are the three things that determine if you have a qualified prospect?

2. How interested does the prospect have to be in your product or service to be "qualified"?

3. What does the Closer use to build the prospect's interest in his product or service?

4. How do you determine for yourself if a prospect is truly qualified?

5. Write a list of several questions that you can ask your prospects to determine if they can: a) use your product or service, b) authorize or obtain authorization for its purchase, and c) pay for it.

6. What should you do after asking a prospect a question?

7. What should you do if you ask a question but the prospect doesn't really answer it?

8. Other than asking questions, what other way can you tell if your prospect is qualified?

9. Describe what mixing qualifying questions with later steps of the 8-Step Road Map means. What's the purpose of doing this?

10. Practice with a friend or co-worker fully qualifying him/her for your product or service. Practice this until you can do it smoothly and confidently.

11. Practice with a friend or co-worker the qualifying step WITH your introduction step included. Practice this until you can do it smoothly and confidently.

5

Thru Ch. 7

you determined whether

essarily wants) your prod-

and has the means to pay

osers) are itching at this

presentation and tell their prospects everything about the product. They are eager to sell their "solution," which, after all, is what they're selling, isn't it?

But there is a vital step missing. They haven't yet established what problems their product or service will solve for that particular prospect. (Or, what desires their product or service will fulfill for that prospect.)

You may (and should) know everything that your product or service can do and all of the problems it can solve, but at this stage, you don't know which *specific* problems or desires *that particular* prospect needs/wants solved or fulfilled. And the prospect might not know, either.

If you don't discover the prospect's problems, how can you know what to say in your presentation?

Without first finding the prospect's problems or desires, Presenters start at the beginning and tell the prospect absolutely everything they know about their product or service. They hope that by the time they've said all they know, the prospect will have worked out for himself which problems he wants solved, which desires he wants fulfilled, and how the product or service will accomplish this for him.

Have you ever had a salesperson talk at you about her product or service for what feels like an eternity, and when she finally runs out of things to say, ask you, "What do you think?"

Did you end up buying from that person? I'll bet you didn't.

A MASTER CLOSER WANTS TO FIND THE PROSPECT'S BIGGEST PROBLEMS, CONCERNS, NEEDS, WANTS, AND DESIRES THAT HE KNOWS HIS PRODUCT OR SERVICE CAN SOLVE AND/OR FULFILL.

The problems or desires affect the prospect personally or his family, career, business, money, future, security, time, and so on, depending on whom you are selling to and what you are selling. They are the entrance point to the sale.

Products and services are solutions. The prospect buys solutions to problems that he wants solved.

The Closer wants to discover the prospect's problems before he starts any presentation for the following reasons:

1) It makes the prospect acutely aware of problems he may not have thought about or cared enough about to want to solve resulting in him being eager to hear the presentation.

2) It tells the Closer how to customize her presentation. She will say only those things about her product or service that solves that prospect's specific problems. This allows the Closer to direct the prospect, keep his attention on the sale, and build interest in the product or service.

3) The Closer can use the problems found and the need to solve them as "hot buttons" to "push" (mention) <u>throughout</u> the sale to move the prospect through his resistance or objections to buying.

It is vital that you really understand what it is that your product or service really provides for the prospect. I'm not talking about just the distinctive features (parts that stand out) of the product or service, but the *benefits* that result from those features that the prospect will enjoy in the end. Remember, people buy solutions to problems and satisfactions of desires—they don't buy a bunch of technical features. The benefit answers the number one question in the prospect's head: *What's in it for me?*

My software company sold certification training courses to technicians. They didn't feel they were just buying courses or training—they knew they were buying career advancement, job security, and higher salaries. They knew that's what they were buying because my salespeople consistently discovered that their prospects desired these things and then showed them how our products helped them fulfill these desires.

The bigger the problem, or the stronger the desire, the easier it is to close the prospect on your product or service (assuming, of course, it really solves those problems or fulfills those desires)

BEFORE A CLOSER WILL SELL PROSPECTS HER SOLUTION, SHE HAS TO FIRST FIND THEIR PROBLEMS.

So how does a Closer find each prospect's unique problems or desires? There are two ways:

1) By asking questions that will uncover them 2) By mentioning problems or desires that the Closer feels may exist

Below is a sampling of the type of questions you can ask.

"What problems do you run into when_____?"

"Is_____ ever a problem for you?"

"Do you have a need to _____?"

"Have you ever wanted _____?"

"Are you ever concerned that_____?"

"How important is it to you that _____?"

"If you could _____, would that be a big benefit to you (or your family, your business)?"

"Would it be a big benefit to you if you were able to _____?"

"Is there a need in your business to _____?"

"Have you ever missed any opportunities to_____ because you _____?"

"What would you like to see improved about what you're using now?"

"What benefits do you look for in _____?"

"What are you looking to achieve when it comes to _____?"

"If you could quickly and cost effectively_____, would that be a big benefit to you?"

When the prospect answers, ask more questions about it until you have fully uncovered the hottest problems, needs, wants, or desires.

Note: Make sure you note down everything that you discover as you will be using it later. After you find more than one problem or desire, ask which one or two are the most vital to be solved or fulfilled. Then use those to carry the prospect through the rest of the sale. This keeps your presentation focused on the strongest selling points.

The other way to find a prospect's problems or desires is by bringing up possibilities and seeing how he responds.

Here is an example of how to point out a hot problem that your product can solve that the prospect really wasn't aware of:

When we sold products to PC and network technicians, we would ask prospects:

"What do you use to diagnose broken PCs?"

Many would say they used trial and error and didn't seem to think that it was a problem.

"How long does it normally take you, on average, to diagnose a broken PC?"

They typically answered anywhere from 30 minutes to several hours. At this point, they still didn't seem concerned about it.

Closer: "How many of those PCs do you run into that take more than a half hour to diagnose?"

Prospect: "Hmmm, more than I would like."

Closer: "Well, what percentage if you had to guess?"

Prospect: "Maybe 30-40%."

Aha! Now <u>that</u> is a problem that the prospect is now aware of, and one that I knew my product solved.

What do you think the odds would be of closing this sale after having zeroed in on this problem? In many cases, that alone was enough to make the technician want to buy our product. As you can imagine, this one little discovery makes the whole sale significantly more favorable than just plowing forward into a presentation without uncovering such a problem, telling everything about the product, and hoping that the prospect will connect the dots himself and want to buy.

Remember, the problem or desire is sometimes below the awareness of the prospect, and the Closer has to point it out and make sure the prospect sees it as a problem.

Here's another example:

A Closer who is selling water purification systems to a prospect who thinks that his tap water is all he needs might have to point out the dangerous chemicals that are added to tap water to make it clean—toxins that his family is being exposed to everyday.

Prospect: "We use tap water."

Closer: "That's fine. Let me ask, are you aware of the recent study that came out about the effects of chlorine and fluoride that are added to the water supply?"

Prospect: "No. What effects?"

Closer: "Well, it's your choice of course, but since you told me you have kids, let me show (or read) you a portion of that study."

Prospect: "Wow, I had no idea!"

The prospect now sees a problem that he didn't know existed.

Closer: "Not only that, but did you know that a recent study has found traces of pharmaceutical drugs in the public drinking supply in 24 major cities?"

Prospect: "I didn't know. That's crazy!"

The prospect is now aware of two problems.

The Closer continues to do this until he feels he has enough hot problems that he knows his product or service will solve. Some prospects will close with only one hot problem solved or one desire met, whereas others may need several. The Closer can always come back to this step and find more problems or desires if her prospect shows a lack of interest at a later point in the sale.

To ensure that you successfully complete this step, make a list of every problem, need, want, desire, ambition, and goal that you can come up with that you know your product or service will solve or provide. You should be able to compile this list either from experience, surveying your customers, and/or by asking your manager or other top Closers at your company. You can use this list to not only create your questions, but to prompt your prospects in case you can't discover their problem with questions alone.

Again, like the Qualify step, keep this step conversational. Don't ask all your questions, one after the other, like it's an interrogation. Also, as mentioned in the previous chapter, you can mix in a couple of qualification questions as needed into this step.

You can also give the prospect a tidbit—but not more than a taste—of what you're going to present to keep him interested as you are digging for the hot problem.

You are providing your prospect with solutions to his needs, wants, desires, goals, and ambitions. You are selling solutions to problems. You have to first find the prospect's problems or desires that you know your product or service will solve or fulfill. Once you have found one or more hot problems that you know your product or service can solve, you're ready to move on to Step 4 of the 8-Step Road Map.

EXERCISES:

Write your answers on a separate piece of paper.

1. What are the three reasons why the Closer wants to discover the prospect's problem or desire before starting any presentation?

2. What are the two ways that a Closer can find the problem?

3. Write out what <u>your</u> product or service provides for your buyer. (This isn't really the features of the product or service, but the benefits of those features. This answers the number one question in the prospect's head: *What's in it for me?*).

4. Why is it a good idea to make a list of every problem and desire that you can come up with that you know your product or service will solve?

5. Make a list of every problem, need, want, desire, and goal you can come up with that you know your product/service will solve/provide. Compile this list either from experience, surveying your customers, and/or by asking your manager or other top Closers at your company.

6. Practice, with a friend or co-worker, finding problems and desires. Use the example questions from this chapter and also come up with your own questions. Make it sound conversational and don't ask all your questions one after the other like it's an interrogation. Practice until you can do this smoothly and confidently.

7. Practice, with a friend or co-worker, finding problems and desires by prompting him/her with the list of problems and desires you created in #5 above. Practice until you can do this smoothly and confidently.

8. Practice, with a friend or co-worker, finding problems and desires and mixing in a couple of qualifying questions. Practice until you can do this smoothly and confidently.

9. Practice with a friend or co-worker finding the problem WITH your introduction and qualifying step included. Practice this until you can do it smoothly and confidently.

6

SET-UP THE PRESENTATION

INTRODUCTION STEP:

You have a prospect who knows who you are, the reason for your call, and that you are there to see if you can be of help and who has agreed to be asked questions.

QUALIFY STEP:

You have determined that the prospect can use your product, can authorize purchasing it, and can pay for it.

FIND THE PROBLEMS STEP:

Through questioning, or prompting, you have uncovered the prospect's specific hot problems that you know your product or service can solve.

You are now ready to give her your best customized presentation, right? Almost—but not quite. You still have an important step to do that will properly set up your presentation.

Remember that selling is a process of getting smaller agreements or closes, which leads to the major final agreement or close (where the prospect finally agrees to the purchase and terms).

There are two specific smaller agreements that a Closer wants to get from the prospect after uncovering the hot problems or desires, before starting a presentation:

1. THE CLOSER WANTS THE PROSPECT TO AGREE THAT THE PROBLEMS OR DESIRES FOUND ARE IMPORTANT AND THAT THEY NEED TO BE SOLVED OR FULFILLED. THE CLOSER <u>SELLS</u> THE PROBLEMS TO THE PROSPECT BEFORE SELLING THE PRODUCT OR SERVICE.

2. THE CLOSER ALSO WANTS THE PROSPECT TO AGREE TO HEAR THE CLOSER'S SOLUTION TO THE PROBLEMS.

The Closer takes the hottest problems and then sells them to the prospect, getting her to really see them as problems. He builds the problems up, making them as personal as he can, and increases the urgency to have them solved.

"So, how is_____ affecting your business (or family, or life)?"

"How big of a problem is that for you?"

"How important is that to you?"

"How long has that been going on?"

"What would it mean to you if you were to achieve that?"

"How long has that been a problem for you?"

BEFORE A CLOSER WILL SELL THE PROSPECT THE SOLUTION HE WILL FIRST "SELL" THE PROSPECT HIS OWN PROBLEM.

Using the example from the last chapter where the technician who fixes computers loses money on some of the PCs because it takes too long to diagnose the problems, the Closer does the following:

Closer: "How does that affect your productivity (revenue, or bottom line)?"

Prospect: "Don't make much money on those…May even lose on some."

Closer: "Oh, what percentage would you say you lose money on?"

Prospect: "Maybe as many as 25%."

Closer: "Wow, and what about the lost opportunity of not having time to take in more business or service more accounts?"

Prospect: "Yeah, that too."

Closer: "So, you're losing money on 25% of the computers you get to fix along with the opportunity costs of not being able to work on more computers?"

Prospect: "Yes."

Closer: "So, if you could reduce the time it takes to debug the cause of PC failure, would that solve a big problem for you?"

Prospect: "Sure!"

Now <u>that</u> is a hot problem that the prospect is now aware of, that the Closer knows his product will solve, and that the prospect wants solved. All that's left is to get the prospect to agree that she wants to know about the Closer's solution.

Because of everything the Closer accomplished in the previous steps, the prospect may be ready to hear the solution, but to be sure, the Closer confirms it by asking:

"So, if I could show you how you could solve (<u>hot problem</u>) would you want to know about it?"

or,

"So if I could show you how you could _____ so that you would solve _____, would you want to know about it?"

Example from scenario above:

"So, if I could show you how you could cut down the time it takes to diagnose a PC so that it would solve the problem of repair jobs that were costing you money, would you want to know about it?"

You get the "yes," and the prospect is now properly set up for Step 5 on the 8-Step Road Map, the Presentation.

While Set-Up the Presentation is its own step done just prior to setting up the *overall* Presentation step, it is also ideally used *during* the presentation to set-up specific features and benefits. This will be explained with examples in the next chapter.

If you found more than one problem, during the Find the Problems step, you also set up each of them again during the Presentation:

"Okay, so you also mentioned you had a problem with _____, right? So, if we can also solve that for you that would be important to you, yes?"

If, during the presentation step, your prospect loses interest, you simply push the hot buttons (problems, needs, desire, etc.) you found earlier and get the prospect to agree again that they are important to solve.

If, at any point after this step in the sale, it appears that the problems you found aren't generating enough interest in the prospect, use questions to probe for another hot problem that the prospect is interested in solving, and that you know your product or service can solve.

EXERCISES:

Write your answers on a separate piece of paper.

1. What are the two smaller agreements (closes) that the Closer wants to get from the prospect after he uncovers the hot problems but before starting the presentation?

2. What does it mean to "build up the problem" and why should you do this?

3. Practice, with a friend or co-worker, building up and "selling" the prospect her problems. You can use the sample scripted wording in this chapter, or create your own to tailor fit your product or service. Do this step until you feel you can do it smoothly and confidently.

4. Practice, with a friend or co-worker, getting the agreement to hear your solution. You can use the sample scripted wording in this chapter or create your own. Do this step until you feel you can do it smoothly and confidently.

5. Practice with a friend or co-worker fully setting up the presentation WITH your introduction, qualifying, and find the problem steps. Practice this until you can do it smoothly and confidently.

7

THE PRESENTATION

A PRESENTATION IS DEFINED SIMPLY as "giving the prospect information about your product or service." This is where you actually sell your solution (product or service.)

That defines the activity, but what is the **purpose** of the presentation?

Is it to educate or enlighten the prospect about what your product or service does? Is it to explain the features and benefits? Is it to show him how good it is?

While the presentation involves these things, they are not its <u>primary</u> purpose.

THE PRIMARY PURPOSE OF THE PRESENTATION IS TO <u>CREATE OPPORTUNITIES</u> TO CLOSE.

That is really the entire purpose of the presentation. There is no other.

A Closer doesn't wait for closing opportunities to magically appear—she creates them. She creates them with her presentation.

A CLOSING OPPORTUNITY IS A MOMENT WHERE THE PROSPECT GIVES A SIGNAL THAT HE MIGHT HAVE ENOUGH INTEREST IN THE PRODUCT OR SERVICE TO BUY IT.

A major difference between a Closer and a Presenter is that the Presenter typically gives a complete presentation and may not create a single closing opportunity or, when she does, she often misses it.

The Closer uses the presentation as a tool to create closing opportunities (buying signals), recognize them, and immediately go for the close.

The Closer rarely gives an A-Z presentation, rattling off all possible features (the 'things') and benefits (what the prospect gains from the features) hoping that, by the end, the prospect is interested in buying.

The Closer crafts, or customizes, her presentation according to what hot problems or needs she found in the prospect. She knows which features of her product or service will solve the problems that the prospect wants solved and which benefits will most appeal to him.

The Closer doesn't waste time discussing features and benefits that have nothing to do with the prospect's problems or desires. This way, she keeps the prospect's attention and continues to build more and more interest in the product or service, rather than bore and ultimately lose the prospect by talking about things he doesn't care about.

Every time the Closer gives a feature of her product or service, she then makes sure that the prospect also knows the benefit of that feature. The prospect may or may not understand or care about the feature, but will care what the *benefit* will be that he'll get from that feature.

Example of features and their benefits if you are selling a sports car:

FEATURES	BENEFITS
400 hp turbo engine	Neck breaking acceleration
Stiff suspension	Handles like a race car
Ceramic composite brakes	Superior stopping power
Beautiful exterior styling	People will take notice

The Closer doesn't assume that the prospect will automatically see the benefit from the features he mentions. The Closer doesn't leave it up to the prospect to convert the features into benefits, but instead does it for him by adding, "which means you____" after stating each feature.

"Our product has (feature), *which means you* (benefit).*"*

Example:

"This car comes with a turbocharged 400 hp engine which means you will experience neck-breaking 0-60 acceleration in less than 4 seconds."

The prospect is buying the benefits of features. He may recognize the benefits on his own, but the Closer makes sure of it. She makes sure that the features and benefits presented are only those that help solve the prospect's problems or fulfill his desires.

For every product or service you sell, you should have a "reasons to buy" list. List in one column every feature of your product or service; in a column next to it, list out all of the benefits that the prospect will get from each feature. You should know the list cold—I recommend that you practice it by speaking it aloud over and over until you can rattle them off without even thinking about it.

ALWAYS GIVE THE BENEFITS WHEN MENTIONING FEATURES. FEATURES SHOULD RARELY BE PRESENTED ALONE.

If, during the presentation, you can't generate much interest despite sharing features and benefits that align with the problems you discovered earlier, or if the sale later stalls and you're at loss of what to do, then you may not have found hot enough problems or desires for that prospect. Go back and reconfirm that the problems or desires that the prospect told you are actually important to him. Sometimes all you have to do is push those buttons a few times to get the prospect interested in your presentation.

Example:

Closer: "I know you mentioned earlier that _____ is a big concern of yours, right?"

Prospect: "Yes."

Closer: "And it's been a problem for some time, yes?"

Prospect: "Yes."

Closer: "And that's costing you money daily by not having it solved, correct?"

Prospect: "Yes."

Closer: "How much, if you had to guess, would you say you're losing daily by not having this solved?"

Prospect: "Probably thousands."

Closer: "So, if my product/service could fix this for you at a cost-effective price, you would want to know how it could be done, right?"

Prospect: "Yes, of course."

Closer: (Back to presentation)

If that doesn't do it, then dig deeper with questions to discover other, bigger problems or desires that will grab the prospect's interest. With new, hot problems, do the Set-Up the Presentation and Presentation steps again, aligning it to the new problems or desires.

"Let me ask you, other than _____, what other problems are you running into that_____?"

or,

"Let me ask you, aside from_____, what else are you looking to achieve regarding _____?"

Features and benefits that solve the prospect's problems or desires make up the essence of the Closer's presentation. However, as I mentioned in the previous chapter, the Closer ideally sets up each feature/benefit before presenting them.

The components and sequence of the Presentation include:

PROBLEM → SET-UP → SOLUTION (Feature) → BENEFIT

Here is an example of all these components being used in a Closer's presentation of selling a car. It was found out earlier, from the Find the Problems step, that *safety* was the biggest concern of the prospect, and the Closer knows the car he is selling has three features that can solve the prospect's concern:

"Okay, so you mentioned safety was your major concern [**Problem found earlier**]. *And, you said that you were in a really bad accident when you were younger, and I'm sure you don't want to ever experience anything like that again* [**Set-Up: built up the problem**]. *So, having a car that you know you and your family will be safe in is something that you would want, right?"* Yes. [**Set-up: wants solution**].

"So, let's talk about the safety features. Have you ever been in a situation where your brakes, after riding them in stop and go traffic, 'fade' and don't work as strong?" Yes. [**This is a new problem, related to the problem of *safety*, the Closer points out**].

"Well, that's called brake fade and can result in not having enough stopping power ending up in a collision [**Set-Up: built up the problem**]. *So, if you had a car with brakes that never fade, I'm sure that's something you'd want, yes?"* Yes. [**Set-Up: wants solution**].

"Well, this car you're looking at comes with ceramic disk brakes [**First feature**], *which means to you that your brakes will never fade and you will be able to stop your car reducing the chance for an accident and injury* [**Benefit**].

"Now, have you ever been distracted while driving, like talking on a cell phone (or texting) and almost get into an accident?" Yes. [**New problem, related to the problem of *safety*, the Closer points out**].

"Obviously, that can be potentially life threatening to you and your family [**Set-Up: built up the problem**]. *And, if you could be alerted to this to prevent an accident, that would be important to you?"* Yes. [**Set-Up: wants solution**].

"Well, this car comes equipped with a state-of-the-art laser warning device that will warn you whenever this happens [**Second feature**], *which means you will be able to take action and prevent a life threatening accident* [**Benefit**].

"Now, you also mentioned you have small children. I assume that they often drive with you in the car?" Yes. [**New problem, related to the problem of *safety*, the Closer points out**].

"And, I'm sure if you were in a collision [**Set-Up: built up the problem**], *knowing that your kids were in the safest car possible, is something you'd want as well, right?"* Yes. [**Set-Up: wants solution**].

"That's why we have 10 air bags, with 5 in the back [**Third feature**], *which means you and your kids will have the greatest amount of protection against injury* [**Benefit**]."

The above example would be the ideal, but is not easy to achieve on the fly until you have lots of practice or experience doing it. However, you should strive to include as many of these elements as possible. I recommend that you script this out it in advance with the various set of features that you might use in future presentations and practice until you can do it perfectly.

The next chapter discusses one final component that a Closer adds to the presentation (Step 6 of the 8-Step Road Map) to proactively create buying signals and closing opportunities.

EXERCISES:

1. What is the definition of the word, "presentation"?

2. What is the purpose of the presentation?

3. What is a closing opportunity?

4. What does the Closer use the presentation for?

5. What is the difference between a feature and a benefit?

6. How do Closers craft their presentations?

7. Create a list of reasons to buy your product or service. In one column list the features and in the next column, the benefits of the features.

8. Practice, with a friend or co-worker, converting the features into benefits as described in this chapter. Do this step until you can do it smoothly and confidently.

9. Practice, with a friend or co-worker, going back and reconfirming that the problems are actually important. Push the "hot buttons" to raise interest in your presentation. Do this step until you can do it smoothly and confidently.

10. Practice, with a friend or co-worker, digging to see if there are other, bigger problems or desires that will grab his or her interest. With the new problems or desires, do the Set-Up the Presentation and Presentation steps again, ensuring to align them to the new problems or desires. Do this step until you can do it smoothly and confidently.

11. What are the components of the presentation and their sequence?

12. Script out your presentation with all possible features and include all the components of the presentation in their proper sequence. Note: Even though you will very rarely ever give your presentation with all possible features, you still want to have them all scripted out so you can practice them.

13. Practice, with a friend or co-worker, giving your presentation using all the components in the proper sequence. Practice all possible features of your product or service. Do this step until you can do it smoothly and confidently.

14. Practice with a friend or co-worker giving your presentation WITH your introduction, qualifying, find the problem and setting up the presentation steps included. Practice this until you can do it smoothly and confidently.

8

HOW TO CREATE OPPORTUNITIES TO CLOSE

THE CLOSER CREATES CLOSING OPPORTUNITIES with his presentation by getting a series of smaller agreements from the prospect regarding the solution he is selling. He gets the prospect to agree that the features and benefits of his product or service will help solve the prospect's problems or desires found during Step 3.

The Closer gets the prospect to agree to key statements about his product or service by asking a question afterward, to which the prospect answers "yes."

Example:

Closer: "Our diagnostic product runs a complete battery of tests on a PC and reports the exact trouble spot, which means you don't waste time with trial and error, <u>which has been a big problem on several of your jobs, hasn't it?</u>"

Prospect: "Yes."

Closer: "The whole process takes just about 5 minutes, which means you can cut your diagnostic time down to a fraction. <u>Can you see how this will allow you to fix more PCs in less time?</u>"

Prospect: "Yes."

Closer: "And that means more revenue per hour, <u>doesn't it?</u>"

Prospect: "Yes."

Closer: "<u>That would be a big benefit for you and the company?</u>"

Prospect: "Yes."

THIS SERIES OF AGREEMENTS FORM A YES-PATTERN AND BUILDS INTEREST IN THE PRODUCT OR SERVICE. THIS YES-PATTERN DOESN'T OCCUR ON ITS OWN. THE CLOSER USES THE PRESENTATION AS A TOOL TO CREATE IT, IN TURN CREATING OPPORTUNITIES TO CLOSE.

Without the question tacked on at the end of each statement (commonly called "Tie-Downs"), there is no guarantee of getting agreement to them. Read again the example above, this time omitting the underlined parts (the Tie-Downs), and notice the difference.

There are many ways to tie down an agreement and get a "yes."

Examples of Tie-Downs:

"Do you see how this would be a big benefit to you?"

"That's going to be a big help, isn't it?"

"See how that will help you?"

"Does that sound good?"

"Sound good?"

"Does that make sense?"

"Make sense?"

"Right?"

"Isn't it?"

"Wouldn't it?"

"Doesn't it?"

"Would you agree?"

"Can you see that?"

"That's what you're looking for, isn't it?"

Here is the same example of the Closer's presentation (selling a car), from the last chapter, but with the addition of Tie-Downs as the final added component to create a Yes-Pattern and closing opportunity:

"Okay, so you mentioned safety was your major concern. And, you said that you were in a really bad accident when you were younger, and I'm sure you don't want to ever experience anything like that again. So, having a car that you know you and your family will be safe in is something that you would want, **right?***"* **Yes.**

"So, let's talk about the safety features. Have you ever been in a situation where your brakes, after riding them in stop and go traffic, 'fade' and don't work as strong?" Yes.

"Well, that's called brake fade and can result in not having enough stopping power ending up in a collision. **Make sense?***"* **Yes.** *"So, if you had a car with brakes that never fade, I'm sure that' something you'd want,* **yes?***"* **Yes.**

"Well, this car you're looking at comes with ceramic disk brake which means to you that your brakes will never fade and you will be able to stop your car reducing the chance for an accident and injury. **Do you see how this would be a big benefit to you?***"* **Yes.**

"Now, have you ever been distracted while driving, like talking on a cell phone (or texting) and almost get into an accident?" Yes.

"Obviously, that can be potentially life threatening to you and your family. **Do you agree?"** Yes. *"And, if you could be alerted to this to prevent an accident, that would be important to you,* **am I right?"** **Yes.**

"Well, this car comes equipped with a state-of-the-art laser warning device that will warn you whenever this happens, which means you will be able to take action and prevent a life threatening accident. When it comes to safety, that's another huge benefit, **isn't it?"** Yes.

"Now, you also mentioned you have small children. I assume that they often drive with you in the car?" Yes.

"And, I'm sure if you were in a collision, knowing that your kids were in the safest car possible, is something you'd want as well, **am I right?"** Yes.

"That's why we have 10 air bags, with 5 in the back, which means you and your kids will have the greatest amount of protection against injury. **Can you see how this will keep your kids safe?"** Yes.

Again, the above example would be the ideal, but requires practice to master it. But, adding Tie-Downs to your presentation is vital to creating closing opportunities, wouldn't you agree?

Sometimes you need to use Double Tie-Downs to get a firm agreement from the prospect:

"That's why we have 10 air bags with 5 in the back which means you and your kids will have the greatest amount of protection against injury. **Can you see how this will keep your kids safe?"** Yes.

"I mean that's the most important thing to you, **would you agree?"** **Yes!**

You can also use Tie-Downs to wrap up a series of features/benefits for each separate problem that you solve before going onto the next:

"So can you see how ceramic disc brakes, the laser warning system and the 10 airbags **will be a big benefit to you?"** Yes. *"And they fully handle your concern about safety?"* **Yes!**

MOMENTUM SELLING

The Closer uses Tie-Downs and creates a Yes-Pattern to build momentum that is hard for the prospect to resist as they move toward the close.

Momentum means "a driving force gained through motion." Try punching the palm of one hand with your fist from the other hand only 1 inch away. Not a lot of impact, is there? Now throw that punch from 12 inches away. Boom! That's a driving force. Just like a pole vaulter who needs a running start to leap over the bar, you need to build momentum before going for the close. You do this by getting the prospect to agree to key statements, and thus establishing a Yes-Pattern.

GAINING AGREEMENTS = BUILDING MOMENTUM

The more your prospect agrees, the more momentum you're building. Each agreement is a *small* or *minor* close that is necessary to obtaining the *final close*.

USING TIE-DOWNS AFTER KEY STATEMENTS TO GAIN AGREEMENTS AND BUILD THE YES-PATTERN IS THE PRIMARY WAY TO CREATE BUYING SIGNALS AND CLOSING OPPORTUNITIES.

WHEN A PROSPECT ASKS A QUESTION

Most prospects will ask questions during some portion of the sale, particularly during the presentation. If the questions are sincere and related to solving her problems or to your product/service, this is a good sign that the prospect is really listening and is interested and engaged in the sales process.

The Closer welcomes these questions, and when they arise, temporarily gives the prospect control of the sale. This is fine as long as the Closer, after answering, regains control and continues to build momentum and direct the prospect along the 8-Step Road Map.

To regain control, the Closer can ask his own question after answering the prospect's. He doesn't, however, answer the prospect's question and then sit silently as this offers control of the sale to the prospect, which risks losing momentum due to the prospect losing interest or coming up with reasons not to buy (objections).

The Closer always tries to use his answers to questions to continue to build a Yes-Pattern. He then returns to the step of the road map that he is on. If the question is asked during the close step, the Closer answers and resumes closing.

A SUCCESSFUL CLOSER NEVER LOSES SIGHT OF WHERE HE IS ON THE ROAD MAP, AND ALWAYS GETS BACK ON TRACK AS QUICKLY AS HE CAN.

Example:

Closer: "Our diagnostic product runs a complete battery of tests on a PC and reports the exact trouble spots, which means no more wasted time with trial and error. This has been a big problem on several of your jobs, hasn't it?"

Prospect: "Yes. How long does the test take?"

Closer: "The whole process takes just about 5 minutes, which means you can cut your diagnostic time down to a fraction. Can you see how this will allow you to fix more PCs in less time?"

Prospect: "Yes."

Closer: "And that means more revenue per hour, doesn't it?"

Prospect: "Yes."

The Closer answered the question then immediately asked his own questions to reassume control of the sale and continue to build the momentum of the Yes-Pattern.

A Closer can also confirm he answered the prospect's question to build momentum.

Example:

Closer: "Does that fully answer that for you?"

Prospect: "Yes."

PROSPECTS BELIEVE AUTHORITIES

Whenever possible, you should support your claims about your product or service with a quote from an independent authority that the prospect would respect, and then tie it down to build the Yes-Pattern, and momentum.

For instance, if you are selling a purified water system:

Closer: "Your tap water contains x amount of chlorine and fluoride which means you and your family are at risk of _____. That's something you want to protect your family from, isn't it?"

Prospect: "Yes."

Closer: "Let me share with you a quote from a recent article that was in the ABC Journal that tells exactly what the risk is. (Read a short quote.) Can you see the danger?"

Prospect: "Yes."

You can also use customer testimonials and success stories to build credibility.

So, now you know how to customize your presentation, control the prospect's attention, and direct it to the right features and benefits so the prospect realizes how your product or service solves her problems or desires. You also know how to create opportunities to close during the presentation by using Tie-Down questions to build a Yes-Pattern and momentum.

The next skill to learn is spotting when to close which is Step 7 of the 8-Step Road Map.

EXERCISES:

Write your answers on a separate piece of paper.

1. A Closer uses the presentation to get a series of _____ _____from the prospect regarding the solution he is selling. (Fill in the blanks.)

2. What does the Closer get the prospect to agree to as he does his presentation?

3. How does the Closer get the prospect to agree to the key statements he says about his product or service?

4. What is a Yes-Pattern and how does the Closer create one?

5. What is a Tie-Down?

6. Write down 4-5 examples of Tie-Downs.

7. What is the definition of "momentum," and what is "momentum selling"?

8. What is the primary way a Closer creates buying signals and closing opportunities?

9. Practice, with a friend or co-worker, using Tie-Downs with features and benefits. Do this step until you can do it smoothly and confidently

10. Practice, with a friend or co-worker, giving a customized presentation of your product or service that aligns features and benefits to specific problems or desires and uses Tie-Downs to create a Yes-Pattern. Do this step until you can do it smoothly and confidently.

11. What should a Closer do after he answers a prospect's question?

12. Practice, with a friend or co-worker, answering a question, and then ask your own question to regain control of the sale, and then further build the Yes-Pattern. Do this step until you can do it smoothly and confidently.

13. What should a Closer use to support the claims he makes regarding his product or service?

14. Practice, with a friend or co-worker, supporting claims with authority references and Tie-Downs. Do this step until you can do it smoothly and confidently.

15. Practice with a friend or co-worker giving your presentation (including Tie-Downs) WITH your introduction, qualifying, find the problem and setting up the presentation steps included. Practice this until you can do it smoothly and confidently.

9

WHEN TO CLOSE

YOU NOW KNOW HOW TO CREATE an opportunity to close the sale. What do you do once you have created that opportunity?

YOU STOP THE PRESENTATION AND SMOOTHLY AND QUICKLY MOVE TO THE CLOSING STEP.

Don't bypass the opportunity by continuing your presentation.

Now, in order to do this, you have to know what an opportunity looks like, right?

A CLOSING OPPORTUNITY IS A MOMENT WHERE THE PROSPECT GIVES KEY SIGNALS THAT HE HAS ENOUGH INTEREST IN THE PRODUCT OR SERVICE IN ORDER TO BUY.

A signal is anything that "serves to indicate, point out, or warn."

"Buying Signals" are a prospect's way of pointing out to you he has enough interest in your product or service and can be closed. *Enough* is the key word here: it means "adequate or sufficient for the purpose."

Your purpose is to close a sale, not to necessarily have the prospect fully educated on every feature and benefit of your product or

ORATOR

service and be ecstatic or overjoyed (but that's great if he is). **You only need to create an adequate or sufficient amount of interest that will allow you to close the sale.**

Look for the signals that indicate that there is enough interest. These signals can be subtle like an interested, "Oh?!" or "Hmm!" They can be direct or obvious, "This is what I've been looking for." or, "Okay, I want it!" And they could fall anywhere in between.

There are many variations of Buying Signals:

"Yes, send it to me."

"I really like this."

"Wow! That's interesting."

"I like it."

"That's cool!"

"That's great."

"This is exactly what I've been looking for."

"I could use that."

"We need something like that."

The prospect talks about the things he would do with your product or service if he owned it.

"That would help me _____."

The prospect asks questions that clearly show he is interested in the product or service, such as:

"How do I get this?"

"When could you ship it?"

"How much does it cost?"

"What sizes does it come in?"

"How long does it take to get it delivered?"

"Do you take purchase orders?"

"What's the warranty?"

"What are your terms?"

"Do you have it in (color)?"

Depending on how far you are into your presentation, these could be Buying Signals:

- The prospect expresses satisfaction with your explanation or answer to a question.

- The prospect is satisfied with how you handled his objection.

Buying Signals can be subtle such as:

- The prospect is smiling and nodding with you in your presentation.

- The prospect makes agreeable sounds (*"uh huh, uh huh"*).

- The prospect looks or sounds brighter or more enthused.

And finally, what about a Yes-Pattern?

Isn't that a perfect buying signal? The prospect has agreed to everything and answered 'Yes' whenever you asked a tie-down question to get agreement to a key statement. He's agreed to your statements about the features/benefits and how they will solve his problem or need. This a Buying Signal that a Closer can cause to occur, not wait for.

With all Buying Signals, you must use judgment and factor in how and when the prospect says these things. What is his mood, and what is he responding to when he gives these signals?

For example, if the prospect asks about cost in a friendly manner well into the presentation, it is most likely a Buying Signal. However, the same question asked at the very beginning of the presentation with a bit of a hostile edge is not a Buying Signal, but rather an attempt to derail your presentation.

There's no set time when a Buying Signal can occur. They can occur at any point on the 8-Step Road Map, and you have to be on the lookout for them and spot them when they occur. Don't waste them by bypassing them.

A great basketball player dribbles and moves on the court for one purpose: to create an opportunity to shoot the basket. He doesn't keep dribbling, or passing the ball when he's created a clear shot. Otherwise, he'd never score!

So, if you get a prospect on the phone and he says in his first breath, *"I was just going to give you a call about buying your _____."* You're not going to say, *"Wait, let me tell you more about it first."*

Always be alert for Buying Signals, and always act on them.

Whenever you act on a Buying Signal but it turns out the prospect isn't ready to close, he'll let you know. In those cases, rebound and create another closing opportunity.

Alright, now you know when to close, but <u>how</u> do you close?

Continue on to Step 8 and you will see.

EXERCISES:

Write your answers on a separate piece of paper.

1. What does a Closer do when she has created an opportunity to close?

2. What is a Buying Signal?

3. How much interest in the product or service must you create in the prospect?

4. How does the Closer know that the prospect has enough interest?

5. Give 5 examples of Buying Signals.

6. How can a Yes-Pattern be a buying signal?

7. How is the Closer's judgment involved in deciding if she has a Buying Signal and closing opportunity?

8. What does a Closer do if she went for the close, but the Buying Signal didn't turn out to be valid?

9. Practice, with a friend or co-worker, giving your presentation and spotting Buying Signals – obvious, subtle, and everything in between. Do this step until you can do it smoothly and confidently.

10

HOW TO CLOSE

SO YOU HAVE WHAT APPEARS TO BE A REAL Buying Signal. The purpose of the presentation has been achieved—it's time to stop talking about the product and close the sale! This is final step of the 8-Step Road Map.

You've actually been making closes all through the sales process. You closed the secretary or spouse to get the prospect on the phone or to agree to see you, perhaps closed her for an appointment, closed her on being willing to listen to you and answer questions, closed her on telling you her problems or desires and on wanting to know your solution, perhaps closed her on a follow-up appointment or call, and then closed her on agreeing that your product or service can solve her problem or desire. **The whole process is a series of closes ending with one final close.**

The final close occurs and the selling process is complete when the prospect agrees to purchase your product or service and arranges payment.

There are actually two separate closes that take place on this step:

1. Prospect closed on wanting the product or service.

2. Prospect closed on price and terms.

You can't have #2 without first getting #1. If the prospect isn't closed first on wanting the product or service, she will never close on price and terms.

Now, there are many sales techniques out there for closing a sale. Some are good and work well, while others sound phony and insincere. Regardless of whatever closing techniques you use, your objective is to get the credit card, check, signed contract, or purchase order in your hands so you can then deliver your product or service.

I'm not going to share a collection of closing gimmicks in this book—there are many other books available for that. I am, however, going to share a simple, straight forward, persuasive close that I have used regularly throughout my sales career.

If all the previous steps of the 8-Step Road Map have been done, and you have built momentum by getting a Yes-Pattern, then this close will come across as the natural final step and will be hard for prospects to resist. It can also be tailored to sell any product or service.

In order to be closed on wanting the product or service, the prospect must see and agree that it will solve her problem or satisfies her desire. This is brought about with the presentation and, if not already mentioned by the prospect, is confirmed by the Closer as Final Close #1.

Example:

Closer: "So, can you see how (<u>product or service</u>) *will solve* (<u>problem or desire</u>)?"*

Prospect: "Yes."

Closer: "And you can see how that will be a great benefit to you?

Prospect: "Yes."

Prospect is now closed on the product or service. Final Close #1 is done. Simple. You can use your own wording, but make sure it accomplishes the purpose of the close.

Now onto Final Close #2: price and terms.

For a prospect to agree to the price and terms and ultimately make the purchase, she has to see that the value of the product or service meets or exceeds the price.

At this stage, the Closer should <u>assume</u> that the price and terms will be acceptable to the prospect. Why? The price should be acceptable as long as the prospect is qualified, each step of the 8-Step Road Map up to this point has been properly completed, the prospect is closed on wanting the product or service, and the product or service is reasonably or competitively priced.

The Closer, during his presentation, has built momentum and interest using a Yes-Pattern and has just extended it with two more yeses during Final Close #1. Without a pause, he now uses this momentum and moves into the paperwork or other required data gathering and, at the right moment, mentions the price without any doubt that the prospect will agree and buy.

If the prospect doesn't object to the price, then the sale is made. If she balks, you know that she isn't sold and that more work needs to be done which you will learn how to do in the next chapter.

The Closer, without pausing, after getting the two yeses from Final Close #1, tells the prospect what needs to happen in order for her to get the product or service.

Here's an example of Final Close #1 and #2 together:

Final Close #1:

Closer: "So, can you see how (<u>product/service</u>) will solve (or get) (<u>problem or desire</u>)?"

Prospect: "Yes."

Closer: "And you can see how that will be a great benefit to you?

Prospect: "Yes."

Final Close #2:

Closer: "Great! So here's what we need to do to get you started (or get this into your hands). First, I need your shipping address..." [The Closer fills in the order form and gets all needed information.]

Closer: "Okay, so the (<u>product/service</u>*) lists for $1000 and as a first time buyer, you get a 10% discount, which makes it $900 plus $15.75 for shipping and handling, comes to a total of $915.75. Which credit card would you like to put that on?"*

Be quiet and wait for the answer.

If the prospect asks a simple question like, "When can this get shipped?" Answer and ask for the credit card again.

Closer: "It will ship tomorrow, and you should have it in a few days, sound good?

Prospect: "Yes."

Closer: "Great, and which card would you like to use?"

Note: The Closer says, "Here's what <u>we</u> need to do," and not, "what <u>you</u> need to do." You and the prospect are now a team pushing this sale to a close.

Once you get the card number, read it back and tell the prospect what he can expect to happen next. For example:

"This will ship within the next 24 hours, and you should have it by____. A copy of your invoice and instructions will be included in the package. Betty, we appreciate your business, and be sure to call us if you have any questions, okay?"

Adjust the wording as needed to fit your requirements. It's very important to have a precise close worked out beforehand so you do not stumble or sound uncertain.

TELL THE PROSPECT WHAT TO DO

More important than any wording is the fact that the Final Closes require very positive control, more so here than anywhere else.

ALWAYS TELL OR DIRECT YOUR PROSPECTS WHAT TO DO. NEVER LEAVE IT UP TO HIM.

Imagine if a Presenter is driving a race car, over 200 mph. A turn is coming up, and he takes his hands off the wheel hoping it makes it around the next turn, on its own!

Instead of steering a race car, you're steering a prospect. Don't expect the prospect to make the close for you—just as a race car won't make the turn without your hands on the wheel, pushing and guiding it through.

Example of keeping tight control (closing on the phone):

*Closer: "Okay, so the (*product/service*) lists for $1000 and as a first time buyer, you get a 20% discount, which makes it $800 plus $15.75 for shipping and handling, comes to a total of $815.75. Which credit card would you like to put that on?"*

Prospect: "Oh, my wallet is in the car."

Closer: "That's fine, go ahead and get it and I'll hold on."

At the final close you are not "asking" for the order, but are:

1) Telling the prospect what has to happen to get the product or service delivered.

2) Getting the items of information you need from the prospect such as: order form filled out with shipping address, color, size, quantity, shipping preference etc.

3) Telling the prospect what they'll be getting and the total cost.

4) Getting payment preference (credit card, check, purchase order, etc.).

Create your close so that it fits your circumstances. Write it down and practice it until you can do it from start to finish in an energetic and friendly tone without stumbling or pausing.

ADD-ON SALES

Once prospects are closed (after you have their payment method), if you have additional products, services, or accessories that you know they will benefit from, always try to add them to the order while prospects are at their highest level of interest and are in a buying state of mind.

Example:

Closer: "I want to mention something that will help you with (problem or desire).*"*

or,

"I want to mention one other thing. You told me earlier that you would really like to be able to _____, right?"

Prospect: "Yes."

Closer: "Well, we have _____ that will help you with that by _____. Sound good?"

Prospect: "Yes."

Closer: "It's normally $_____, but as part of this order, I can get that to you for $_____. How does that sound?"

NEGOTIATION

Negotiation is the act of reaching an agreement through discussion and compromise. Compromise is when both sides agree to accept less than they originally wanted.

Sometimes, in order for a sale to close, there may have to be some negotiation and compromise on the price or terms. Many buyers insist on getting the best price possible while others just need an incentive to buy now. Some businesses are not flexible on the price, but may be set up to give away additional products/services, features, accessories, etc. at no extra charge as an incentive.

If your business allows you to selectively offer discounted or free items, then you need to know how to best use them in your negotiation.

A prospect isn't going to agree to pay your price and terms if she isn't first closed on wanting the product or service. Offering discounts or freebies when a prospect isn't sold on wanting your product or service is very rarely, if ever, successful.

Remember the need to balance the scale with one tray for the price and another for all the features and benefits of your product or service (the value)? Even after you've loaded all the features and benefits onto the value tray, the prospect may still see the price as heavier on the other one. You either have to load up more value on the one tray or lighten the price on the other (or make it seem lighter to the prospect).

After you've done everything you can to build more value to justify the price, the prospect still may not see the scale as you do. She still may feel the price tray is too heavy. In this case, the Closer first determines if the prospect sees enough value to "want" the product or service regardless of the price.

Closer: "Putting the price (or cost) aside for a moment, what do you think of the product/service?"

Prospect: "I like it."

Closer: "Can you see how it will solve _____ and be a big benefit to you?"

Prospect: "Sure, I really do want it."

Closer: "So, if the price was right for you, would you be ready to get (product or service) today?"

Prospect: "Yes."

Only <u>after</u> the Closer confirms that the prospect is fully closed on wanting the product or service will he then offer discounts or incentives to get the prospect to buy now.

There is an art to offering incentives so that they are perceived as special and have real value to the prospect. Ideally, the prospect should feel as though she has worked for and has earned the incentive, whether it is a lower price or something added to the sale for free.

There are many ways to achieve this. The following is just one example:

Closer: "So, the price is $5,000 and as I said, I can give you the new customer discount of 10% off to bring it to $4,500. How far off on the price do you think we still are?"

Prospect: "I'd be willing to pay $3,500."

Closer: "$3,500? Unfortunately, that's not going to be possible but I might be able to do better than the $4,500, but it would have to be approved by my manager. I know there's no chance of $3,500, but there might be a slight chance at $4,000. Before I even try, I want to know if I was able to get the $4,000 approved, could you do it?"

Prospect: "Yeah, I would do it for $4,000."

Closer: "Okay, I will see what I can do. Are you going to be available in about a half hour?"

Prospect: "Yes."

Closer: "The call won't go to voice mail will it? You'll take the call?"

Prospect: "Yes."

Closer: "And if I can get this price, then we're going ahead today?"

Prospect: "Yes."

Closer: "Okay, I'll call you back in about 30 minutes."

The Closer calls back:

Closer: "Okay, it took some convincing, but my manager approved the $4,000 on two conditions. One is that you keep the price confidential."

Prospect: "Yeah, no problem."

Closer: "And second, we will get a testimonial in writing from you after you've had a chance to use the product (service) and are happy with it. Is that fair enough?"

Prospect: "Fair."

The prospect now feels that she got the best price she could and feels she earned it by not only negotiating but also by giving something in return. Whenever the Closer gives up something in a negotiation, he has every right to get back something in return.

When you have incentives to induce a prospect to buy now, view them as ammunition to use during the negotiation. Do not fire all your ammo at once or too soon.

For a complete understanding of negotiating, I recommend one of the best books I've read on the subject, "Negotiate to Close" by Gary Karrass.

You have now traveled the 8-Step Road Map and understand the fundamental steps of selling, from the introduction to the close, and how to smoothly move the sale from beginning to end.

We're not done yet, though, because there are hazards that you can encounter along the way. The first is the almighty *objection*—the reason for not buying. How do you handle objections and even use them to create a closing opportunity and help close the sale?

You're about to find out.

EXERCISES:

Write your answers on a separate piece of paper.

1. When does the final close of a sale occur?

2. What are the two steps of the final close?

3. What must happen for a prospect to be closed on wanting the product or service?

4. Practice, with a friend or co-worker, confirming that she is closed on wanting the product or service (Final Close #1). Practice until you can do it smoothly and confidently.

5. What has to happen with the prospect regarding the value of the product or service before she will agree to the price and terms?

6. Why does the Closer assume the price and terms will be acceptable to the prospect?

7. How does the Closer keep the momentum going from Final Close #1 (close on wanting product or service) to Final Close #2 (close on price and terms)?

8. Does the Closer pause between Final Close #1 and Final Close #2? Why or why not?

9. What does a Closer do if he is asked a question in the middle of his close?

10. Why does the Closer say, "Here's what we need to do…" not, "Here's what you need to do…" on Final Close #2?

11. At the final close, the Closer is not asking for the order but is doing what? List the four things.

12. Create your own wording for the full final close, steps #1 and #2, for your product or service. Make the necessary changes to the wording in this chapter to fit your product or service.

13. Practice, with a friend or co-worker, your full final close (steps #1 and #2) as written in #12 above. Practice this until you can do it smoothly and confidently.

14. Practice, with a friend or co-worker, doing an "add-on sale" at the close. Practice this until you can do it smoothly and confidently.

15. Practice, with a friend or co-worker, negotiating the price by properly offering discounts or freebies as an incentive to buy now. Practice this until you can do it smoothly and confidently.

16. Practice with a friend or co-worker the entire Road Map giving your full final close WITH your introduction, qualifying, find the problem, setting up the presentation and presentation (including Tie-Downs) steps included. Practice this until you can do it smoothly and confidently.

11

OBJECTIONS

THE BUILDING BLOCKS OF A CLOSED sale are the steps of the 8-Step Road Map. If a salesperson can fully complete each step with a qualified prospect, he or she will end up with a closed sale.

The obstacle that many salespeople fear the most is the prospects' *objections*—that is, their reasons, arguments, or oppositions against buying.

Ideally, a Closer would be able to direct her prospect through each step of the 8-Step Road Map without any objections from the prospect and close the sale on the first attempt. While this does happen, it doesn't happen very often.

The prospect can come up with nearly endless reasons for not buying:

- He has unanswered questions or needs to know more.

- He is confused about something.

- He may have fears and concerns about spending money.

- He may have been ripped off or burned in the past.

- There's another person involved in the decision.

- He doesn't believe you or like you, or he's upset with you.

- He just isn't convinced and/or wants to think about it.

- He wants to buy from a competitor.

- He thinks it costs too much or doesn't have the money.

- He's having a bad day.

- He has an opinion, belief, or idea about something that conflicts with buying your product.

- He was never really qualified to purchase to begin with.

- He has a negative reaction to being "sold" or spending money.

You name it, and the prospect can use it to try to stop a sale from closing. Some objections are concerns in his mind, while others are actual, real-world circumstances that will have to be solved.

These objections can happen at any time during the sales process, but even more so at the close, when the prospect is being asked to make the purchase. Knowing that objections are part of the sale process and that they will typically occur, a Closer is never surprised or thrown off and is always prepared.

The reason she is never thrown off is that she knows how to handle any objection and get back onto the 8-Step Road Map. She even knows how to use an objection to create closing opportunities.

If you knew how to handle any objection that the prospect could come up with and knew how to turn them into a new closing opportunity, you would never be worried about or put off by objections, but would welcome them instead. Skilled at doing this, a Closer is always confident and positive.

A sale could take many closing attempts. Many salespeople give up after the first attempt, while most others quit after the second. You must be prepared and willing to hang in there and keep going for the close until you get it. Be the Closer!

Your attitude is, "I'll get the close no matter what!" View it as a challenge or game.

When an objection arises, the Closer is always thinking how to handle it as quickly and efficiently as possible, with the focus on getting back onto the 8-Step Road Map to the close. She doesn't want to put any more time into it than what is needed to get it out of the way.

Some objections may be very easy to handle, while others can be a challenge. Regardless, if they are blocking the sale from closing, it is the Closer's responsibility to identify what they are, resolve them, and then close the sale.

The art of handling objections starts with determining how to best respond to them, and that is determined by what type of objections they are and when they occur during the sale.

Some objections can simply be acknowledged that you heard them without any further handling. Many need to be answered, while others require questioning to really understand them enough to where they can be answered in a way that builds momentum and creates a closing opportunity.

Through practice and experience, your judgment will strengthen in deciding which approach is best to take.

OBJECTION HANDLING FORMULAS

There are three formulas (a fixed method of doing something) that you can choose from that will allow you to handle any type of objection.

OBJECTION FORMULA #1:

The simplest formula is:

1.   Acknowledge that you heard what the prospect said.

2.   Continue on the 8-Step Road Map.

There is a category of objections that are not really valid concerns of the prospect, but are more like automatic responses. The prospect may say all sorts of things that, on the surface, sound like something you should get into and resolve, but they are not real concerns or barriers to the sale process.

It is best not to go deep into these as they can actually become bigger and more important in the prospect's mind if you pursue them, and then they won't be resolved easily.

If you use this first formula and keep going on the road map, you will find, in most cases, that the prospect will not bring them up again as they weren't actual barriers to the sale. If one turns out to be a real objection, the prospect will surely bring it up again, and you will have to handle it differently (which is covered in the next formulas).

Some examples of objections to be ignored, or simply acknowledged that you heard them, when they occur (usually early on in the sale):

"I don't want to spend any money."

"The economy is bad."

"I don't have a lot of time."

"I have all I need."

"We're over budget."

"Business has been slow."

"I'm not really interested."

"I don't think this is for me."

"I'm just looking."

You can respond to these types of automatic objections with a short statement that simply acknowledges you've heard them (and nothing more), and then get back to the sale.

"Hmm, Hmm...anyway..." (back to sale)

"Okay...anyway..."

"Got it...anyway..."

"I see...anyway..."

With more valid objections or concerns you can use the same formula, but make the acknowledgment a bit stronger and let the prospect know you heard and got what he said. You're still not getting into answering or handling it. The purpose of this is to make the prospect know you got it, and to end any need for further discussion on it.

Examples:

"Wow....I can see that."

"Okay...I see that."

"Really? I didn't know that...that's fine."

"Sounds tough....wow."

"Right, okay."

"Hmm...yeah...I understand."

"Okay...yup...that could be tough."

"I see...no problem...I hear you."

"Oh, wow....got it....okay."

There are many variations of this that will work. You have to do this with tact, of course—you need to do this courteously and in a way that you would like to be talked to.

Asking the prospect a question after letting him know you've heard what he said will allow you to regain control. *"Oh yeah, I know what you mean. Anyway, let me ask you a question..."*

Occasionally, a prospect will ramble on and on, almost like he's reciting a recording, while you sit and wait to get a word in. If this gets out of hand, you can even go as far as cutting the prospect off and pulling his attention back to wherever it is you are on the road map. Do this by calling out the prospect's name, and it will snap him out of it. Then say something like, *"I get what you're saying. Let me ask you a question..."* or, if you were in the middle of your presentation, pick up where you left off, *"Anyway, as I was saying...,"* and build a Yes-Pattern.

If you were closing when this type of objection was voiced and you feel you didn't lose momentum from handling it, then reorient the prospect back to the close and finish the sale.

If you feel like you lost some momentum, you can direct the prospect's attention back to his hottest problem, get him to agree again that he wants it solved and that your product or service will solve it, and then get back to closing. Incidentally, you can do this at any time during the close if the prospect shows some hesitation. It may be all the push he needs to close.

Many objections you run into, particularly ones you get early on in the sale, will be handled with this first formula. Real issues that need to be addressed typically (but not always) come toward the end of the presentation or during the close, and these will need to be fully answered.

OBJECTION FORMULA #2:

1. Answer the objection.

2. Close.

Before you jump to an answer, be sure to let the prospect voice the objection without cutting him off—even if you know what he's going to say. You might have heard the objection a hundred times and feel compelled to quickly answer, but let the prospect get it fully out so he feels that his concerns are being heard.

Once the prospect has had a chance to ask you his question or voice his objection, you want to answer the objection in a way that builds the momentum of the Yes-Pattern and opens the door to a new Buying Signal.

THE PURPOSE OF ANSWERING AN OBJECTION IS THE SAME PURPOSE OF THE PRESENTATION: TO CREATE A CLOSING OPPORTUNITY.

You do this in the same way as the presentation: by getting the prospect to agree to key statements (using Tie-Downs), thus building momentum and a Yes-Pattern.

Example:

The product being sold is a training course which helps PC/network technicians to pass a certification test. The Closer has attempted to close, and the prospect objects, *"It cost too much."*

The Closer answers: "Well, at first it might appear that the initial cost is high, but when you calculate the amount of additional income you could earn in the long run once you're certified, you'll see that this is really not an expense but an investment, and I know you want to be sure you have the best training method possible.... am I right?"

Prospect: "Yes."

Closer: "Now, a lot of money went into developing this course to really make it the best and most accurate. When you're out in the field, you want to know you have the knowledge you need to handle anything that comes up, don't you?"

Prospect: "Yes, of course."

Closer: "And I'm sure you want to be 100% confident when you walk into the testing center that you'll pass your exam, right?"

Prospect: "Yes, sure."

See how the Closer took the objection and used it to start building momentum with a Yes-Pattern? After she gives an adequate answer to the objection, with Tie-Downs, she can confirm the answer with an additional Tie-Down as part of building momentum.

Closer: "So, does that handle it for you, do you see that the value matches, even exceeds, the price?"

Prospect: "Yes."

Other examples of confirming the answer are:

"Does that answer that for you?"

"Does that resolve that for you?"

"Does that handle it fully for you?"

Your answer should be just enough to handle the prospect's objection so that it's no longer a barrier to the sale. Don't overdo it, or you'll risk losing the momentum (and closing opportunity) you've built up or, even worse, making the objection bigger in the prospect's mind than it already was.

If you were about to close or had attempted to close when the objection came up, and your prospect is now satisfied with your answer to his concerns, it's now time to return to the close step. Don't ask if he has any other questions or concerns. Don't hesitate or pause—just go right to the close.

ONCE YOU OVERCOME THE OBJECTION, AND HAVE FULLY BUILT A NEW YES-PATTERN AND CLOSING OPPORTUNITY, THEN YOU CLOSE!

If you cannot build a sufficient Yes-Pattern with your answer and Tie-Downs, then do so after the answer by getting the prospect to agree to several new key statements about the product or service and its benefits. You can also restate key statements he agreed to earlier and build a Yes-Pattern.

WHENEVER POSSIBLE, USE YOUR ANSWER TO BUILD A YES-PATTERN AND CREATE A CLOSING OPPORTUNITY.

It should go without saying, but your answer should always be honest and truthful. Never lie or misrepresent what your product or service can do.

An alternative to answering the objection is asking the prospect, "How do you think you can you solve that?" This works well for objections such as:

"I don't have the money."

"It's not in the budget."

"My wife (boss, partner, accountant etc...) said to hold off."

The prospect often gives problems while the Closer gives solutions. You have to persist with being able to give more solutions than the prospect can give problems. Your solution might not even be the one the prospect finally accepts but he may suddenly become solution oriented and come up with his own solution to his objection. This is why a Closer must have 3-5 answers prepared for each type of objection.

OBJECTION ANSWER HANDBOOK

When I had my sales company, I had the top sales managers and top salespeople list out every objection they had encountered with prospects.

After collecting all the objections and compiling them, I handed the master list back to the same salespeople and managers and asked them to write down how they answer each objection on the list.

The most effective of those answers were then compiled into an "Objection Answer Handbook," and I gave a copy to the entire sales team. They were then equipped with multiple, field-tested answers to every objection they could encounter. I had them memorize at least 2-3 answers for each objection, and then practice plugging those answers into the objection formulas #2 and #3.

With the formulas and the handbook of answers, my salespeople became expert at taking any objection that could come up and turning it into a closing opportunity.

I recommend that you create your own "Objection Answer Handbook" that is unique to your product or service, ensuring that you compile <u>several</u> answers for each objection—not just one.

OBJECTION FORMULA #3 (THE CLOSER'S FORMULA):

This is the formula that the Closer relies on most to handle legitimate objections that come up well into the presentation or at the close. It has two added steps that narrow down the exact, actual objection and help set up the Closer's answer for a sure close.

1. Question the objection.

2. Isolate the objection and set up the close.

3. Answer the actual objection.

4. Close.

THE PURPOSE OF THIS FORMULA IS TO ISOLATE THE REAL OBJECTION AND CREATE AN OPPORTUNITY TO CLOSE.

1. Question the objection.

Knowing the <u>exact</u> reason for not buying is vital to handling it. In many cases, the objection the prospect just stated is not the real reason for not buying.

Sometimes, while well into the presentation or close, the prospect doesn't reveal a specific reason, only that he doesn't want to go ahead and buy. If you don't have the prospect's real reason for not buying, then your answer is not likely to resolve anything and might make things worse instead.

Once the actual reason is uncovered the Closer can then work to resolve it.

Examples of questioning after hearing the prospect's objection:

"Why?"

"Why is that?"

"How come?"

"Why do you feel that way?"

"How exactly is that a problem for you?"

"Can you tell me a little more to make sure I fully understand?"

"What's holding you back?"

"How much too much?"

"That's fine. What is it you still need to think over (or that you're not sure about)?"

You can also simply feed the objection back to the prospect as a question to get him to elaborate:

Prospect: "I want to hold off."

Closer: "You want to hold off??"

You want to question the prospect about his objection for the following reasons:

a. In some cases, the prospect will look at it and solve it himself, or realize it isn't really important, without any further handling from you. This saves a lot of time.

Example:

Prospect: "It costs too much."

Closer: "It costs too much??"

Prospect: "Well, it seems more expensive than your competitors, although you have more features and yours looks like it will last longer...okay, so the price might be worth it."

b. Some objections may be too general to overcome.

By questioning them, you can get more understanding and something specific to handle.

Example:

Prospect: "I'm not interested."

Closer: "How come?"

Prospect: "Well...it sounds good but seems a bit expensive."

Example:

Prospect: "It's not for me."

Closer: "Why is that?"

Prospect: "I'm leaning toward the model your competitor is offering."

Example:

Prospect: "I want to think about it."

Closer: "That's fine. What is it that you're not sure about?"

Prospect: "What if I get it and I don't like it?"

c. A lot of objections you hear are not the actual or real objection. The real objection lies underneath. By questioning it, the prospect will eventually state the real one.

Example:

Prospect: "It's not in the budget."

Closer: "That's fine. Let me ask you just so I understand: If the budget wasn't an issue, what do you think of the software program?"

Prospect: "Oh, I'd like to get it, but I guess my real worry is the time it will take to learn how to use it."

In this case, the real objection wasn't actually the budget, and trying to handle that wouldn't have resulted in a close.

It may take you multiple questions and some digging until you have the actual, specific objection.

The prospect may not have a specific objection other than he just isn't fully convinced. In these cases, some earlier step from the 8-Step Road Map usually needs to be completed or fixed.

Maybe the prospect isn't really convinced that he has a need or problem that he wants resolved, or that your product or service will resolve it. He may not think that your product or service is better than what he is currently using (or a competitor he's considering). He might not be convinced that the value of your product or service meets or exceeds the price.

You can directly ask the prospect about each of the above possibilities (along with other reasons) to find out what the actual objection is. There's always some concrete reason behind "not interested," "not convinced," "not sure," "not now," and so on.

Those types of objections indicate that earlier road map steps may be incomplete and still need handling, so the Closer would revisit that step until the prospect is convinced or interested, and would then follow the 8-Step Road Map again from there to the close.

In many cases, it doesn't take more than reminding the prospect what he agreed to earlier in the sale, getting him to firmly agree to it again, and carrying on rebuilding momentum toward the close.

The most important thing is to dig until you find a specific, real objection.

After you have a specific objection, it often helps to rephrase it in a way that makes it easier for you to resolve it.

Example:

Closer: "When you say 'it costs too much,' is it more that you don't see the value than it is the price?"

Prospect: "Yes. It seems a lot to pay for what I will get."

The Closer now knows that he has to build more value to justify the price.

So, step #1 in this formula is to question the objection until you have a specific, real issue to address. Let's move on to the next step.

2. **Isolate the objection and set up the close.**

a.   By "isolate the objection," I mean you need to determine that it is the <u>only</u> objection standing in the way of closing the sale now. If you don't isolate and zero-in on <u>the</u> objection, you can be expertly handling one objection while the prospect may be looking for and giving you another one. And then another one. And yet another one! You want to know, before answering the first objection, that this is the only real objection.

b.   You set up the close by getting the prospect's agreement that if you can resolve (or handle, or answer) this one objection to his satisfaction, he will then buy.

Examples of how to isolate the objection:

"Okay, so other than (<u>objection</u>), is there any other reason you wouldn't go ahead and get this today?"

or,

"I see. Other than (<u>objection</u>), is there anything else that makes you uncomfortable (you're concerned about, would keep you from moving ahead with this)?"

You can also come up with your own wordings that will determine if this is the only objection, or if there are others.

If the prospect gives you more than one objection, note them all down and ask him which one is most important. He may have more than one valid objection, but there will always be one that is the primary and most important, which you will handle first. In many cases, once you handle the most important one, the others will no longer need to be handled and can be ignored.

Once you have the prospect's main objection and his agreement that it is the most important objection that is keeping him from buying, you then want to set up the close.

Examples:

"So, if I can show you how we could fully handle that, so it won't be a problem, would you then go ahead with this?"

or,

"So, If I could show you how I can fully handle that concern for you, so it isn't a problem, would you be ready to place an order?"

or,

"Oh, so if that wasn't a problem, you'd go ahead?"

You want the prospect's agreement that, if you handle that objection, he will then buy. This helps close the door on him bringing up other objections later on.

3. Answer the Actual Objection.

Once you have found the actual objection and have understood it by questioning, and have an agreement from the prospect that it's the only objection and once it's handled he will buy, it's time to answer the objection.

Now you can plug in your answer as discussed in Formula #2.

There can be several ways to answer objections, and you need to have more than one answer for each objection that you run into. You need to know more reasons to buy than the prospect has reasons not to buy.

4. Close!

ONCE YOU OVERCOME THE OBJECTION AND YOU'VE BUILT A YES-PATTERN AND CLOSING OPPORTUNITY, THEN YOU CLOSE!

If the close is unsuccessful, then dig for another objection and handle as above. Be prepared and willing to do this as many times as needed until you finally get the close.

If necessary, go back and reconfirm the earlier problem or desire that you found (or find another problem or desire) and re-build the momentum with a new Yes-Pattern.

Here are the formulas again:

Objection Formula #1:

1. Acknowledge what the prospect said.

2. Continue on the 8-Step Road Map.

Objection Formula #2:

1. Answer the objection.

2. Close.

Objection Formula #3:

1. Question the objection.

2. Isolate the objection and set up the close.

3. Answer the actual objection.

4. Close.

These formulas will become more effective as you get better at using them. Keep a copy of them on your desk. Practice and use them every day. Adjust the wordings as needed, but stick to the formulas. You should know them so well that they become second nature so you can handle any kind of objection and turn it into an opportunity to close the sale. When a Closer knows she can handle any objection that can come up and turn it into a chance to close the deal, she is truly a Master Closer.

EXERCISES:

Write your answers on a separate piece of paper.

1. What is an objection?

2. Why is a Closer never thrown off when she hears an objection from a prospect?

3. What must your attitude be about handling objections?

4. What is a Closer always thinking when an objection arises?

5. What does the 'art' of handling an objection start with?

6. What is a formula?

7. What is Objection Formula #1?

8. What type of objections is best handled by Objection Formula #1?

9. Practice, with a friend or co-worker, Objection Formula #1. Include getting control back when a prospect is babbling on and on about a non-valid objection. Practice this until you can do it smoothly and confidently.

10. What is Objection Formula #2?

11. How does a Closer answer an objection?

12. What is the Closer's purpose for answering an objection?

13. Practice, with a friend or co-worker, Objection Formula #2. Build a Yes-Pattern, confirm the answer, and then close. Practice this until you can do it smoothly and confidently.

14. What are the four steps to Objection Formula #3?

15. What is the purpose of Objection Formula #3?

16. What are the three reasons a Closer questions an objection?

17. What is the purpose of isolating the objection?

18. What does a Closer do if the prospect gives her more than one objection?

19. What does it mean to "set up the close?"

20. Why should a Closer know more than one answer to an objection?

21. How many times should a Closer be willing to try to close the sale?

22. Practice, with a friend or co-worker, "questioning the objection" (step #1 of Objection Formula #3) so that you can a) get the prospect to answer or resolve the objection himself, b) get down to a specific objection, or c) get to the real objection. Practice situations for a, b and c above until you can do each one smoothly and confidently.

23. Practice, with a friend or co-worker, isolating the objection and setting up the close (step #2 of Objection Formula #3). Practice this until you can do it smoothly and confidently.

24. Practice, with a friend or co-worker, the complete Objection Formula #3. Practice all 4 steps. Practice this until you can do it smoothly and confidently.

25. Create your own "Objection Answer Handbook" as described in this chapter.

12

THE PROSPECT'S COMFORT ZONE

YOUR JOB AS A CLOSER IS TO GUIDE, DIRECT, and push (as needed) a prospect to the close.

A Closer knows he's going to have to be persistent and often push his prospect through the expected resistance in order to close. He is willing to do this <u>only</u> if he believes that the prospect will benefit from his product or service.

The amount of pushing that's needed varies from prospect to prospect and the Closer uses his judgment to determine what is proper. Ideally, the Closer uses just the right amount of force or push—not too little and not too much. The right amount is that which the prospect barely notices, if at all, and that makes her a buyer. Sometimes, however, a Closer inadvertently pushes too hard and drives the prospect out of her "comfort zone."

The prospect's comfort zone is a state wherein she feels secure, comfortable, and in control. Comfort zones vary from prospect to prospect—some people are rarely, if ever, affected by the pressure that can naturally occur during a sale; other people get upset easily, even to the point where they may be unwilling to continue the sale.

Prospects outside of their comfort zones are much harder to

close (if not impossible), but keep in mind that people sometimes need a bit of an extra push to get over their fears and concerns. The Closer can't be afraid of moving prospects out of their comfort zones to help them overcome such fears or concerns, but must develop good judgment on what is just enough and what is too much.

If the Closer does push too far, he knows how to repair it and return the prospect to her comfort zone so that the sale can continue. Knowing this, the Closer doesn't have to hold back and be 'too careful'.

Here is the formula to help resolve upset prospects and get them back into their comfort zone:

1. SPOT IT

You need to be able to quickly spot when the prospect is far enough out of her comfort zone that the sale is at risk of being lost completely.

The prospect may tell you when she's upset. If she does not, there are signs that can indicate that she is out of his comfort zone:

- Tense

- Anxious

- Hostile

- Disagreeable

- Argumentative

- Rude

- Bored or withdrawn

- Angry

- Sarcastic

- Critical

- Agitated or nervous

2. STOP SELLING

You need to use your judgment to decide if the above signs indicate that the prospect is truly upset, or if it is only something mild (or temporary) that can be ignored.

If it's obvious to you that something is going on with the prospect, then <u>stop selling</u>. Continuing on and ignoring upset prospects will usually result in them stopping the sale altogether.

3. RESOLVE THE UPSET

The best way to do this is to:

a) Simply point out to the prospect that you noticed that she may be upset.

b) Let the prospect tell you about it (vent).

c) Apologize (if the upset has to do with you or the sale).

Example:

Closer: "Mary, I could be wrong on this, but I'm getting the impression (or feeling) that you might be a little upset (or uncomfortable) with me?"

Prospect: "Yeah, I've told you that if I'm interested, I'll call you. You're pressuring me, and I just don't like high pressure salespeople."

Closer: "I hear you. First, let me apologize for that...you're right... sometimes I can get carried away and get caught up in the excitement of selling. My intention is not to pressure you into buying. I just want to make sure you have an opportunity to hear all the benefits and have a chance, if you want to take advantage of my product (service)...and again, I do apologize...ok?"

Chances are that in the middle of your apology the prospect will calm down, feel relieved, and tell you it is okay.

Prospect: "Its okay, no big deal."

She's back in her comfort zone.

Closer: "Great, so I wanted to ask you..."

4. RESUME SELLING

Go back to the step you were on, build momentum, and then close.

So, in summary: Spot it. Stop selling. Resolve it. Resume selling.

Sometimes you have to completely change subjects and move onto something else. No matter how upset a prospect has gotten, she can be handled either then or later.

With the 8-Step Road Map, you are changing the prospect into a buyer. The mere fact that she knows you are "selling" her can make her resistive. The Closer knows that this is part of the game and is up for the challenge. He knows, while being persistent, to <u>always</u> be professional, cheerful, and interested in the prospect.

The fact is that selling is not really for the timid. Although many have started their sales careers being timid and fearful, those who gain success, through practice and experience, end up being confident and certain. A Closer does not back off when it comes to contacting, guiding, and pushing a prospect to the close, even if that requires the Closer to widen his <u>own</u> comfort zone to do so.

THE NUMBER OF TIMES THAT YOU CAN CREATE CLOSING OPPORTUNITIES AND ACT ON THEM WITHOUT GIVING UP ON OR UPSETTING THE PROSPECT WILL DETERMINE YOUR NUMBER OF SALES.

EXERCISES:

Write your answers on a separate piece of paper.

1. Why does a Closer have to be persistent and often push his prospect to get a close?

2. How much force or push should the Closer ideally use to make a sale?

3. What is meant by the prospect's "comfort zone?"

4. What happens when a prospect is pushed out of his or her comfort zone?

5. Why is a Closer not overly concerned about the prospect getting pushed out of her comfort zone?

6. What is the formula to handle a prospect who is pushed out of her comfort zone?

7. Practice, with a friend or co-worker, handling a prospect who is pushed out of his or her comfort zone. Practice this until you can do it smoothly and confidently.

13

CALL-BACKS

A "CALL-BACK" IS A SECOND (OR THIRD, FOURTH, and so on) call placed (or visit made) to a prospect who has not yet bought your product or service.

Many businesses have products or services that allow a Closer to get the prospect through the 8-Step Road Map and closed all in one call or visit. There are also many products/services and situations that require one or more call-backs in order for a close to occur.

Regardless if the product or service requires only one or multiple contacts, the Closer is always working to get the prospect as far along the 8-Step Road Map as possible and, if feasible, closed on that call or visit.

Following are some of the common circumstances that create a need for a call-back:

1. The prospect wants to see additional information on your product or service, such as a brochure, web site, fax, catalogue, sample, or demo.

2. The prospect needs to get approval from a spouse or boss.

3. The call is interrupted and can't be completed.

4. The prospect hasn't bought and hasn't been called in a while.

5. The prospect became a customer at some time in the past and is a prospect for buying again.

6. The Closer can't close the prospect on that call or visit for whatever reason, and another attempt is needed.

TRIAL CLOSE

When a Closer manages to get into her presentation on her first call or visit but, for whatever reason, has to end without a final close, she should use a "trial close" before ending to test the water and see where the prospect is at.

Examples:

"Based on what you know so far, does this sound like something that you could benefit from?"

or,

"Based on what you know so far, what do you think of the product (service)?"

or,

"On a scale of 1-10, 10 being you're ready to order, where would you say you are at?...Ok, so what do we have to do to make you a 10?"

If the prospect needs to get approval from someone else to make a purchase:

"If this decision was only up to you, where do you stand? Are you ready to get this?"

The above will give you a good gauge of where the prospect is at before you end the call (or visit).

Chances are that the prospect's interest level will have dropped by the next call or visit, so the Closer doesn't assume that a prospect who's interested at the end of the first call or visit will remain that way until the next encounter. The Closer is always prepared to re-build the interest.

The Closer makes note of what has occurred on each call (or visit) and takes care to include the prospect's problems, desires, and objections. She also notes how far along she moved the prospect on the 8-Step Road Map and how much interest was built (if any). She then uses those notes to craft her call-back introduction before making contact again.

THE CLOSER'S OBJECTIVE ON THE CALL-BACK INTRO-DUCTION IS TO GAIN CONTROL AND START TO BUILD MO-MENTUM AGAIN.

The Closer quickly reorients the prospect to the last call and, without pausing, takes control and begins to build, or rebuild, momentum (see Chapter 8: How to Create Opportunities to Close) with a Yes-Pattern so she can then close.

IN MANY CASES, YOU CAN SIMPLY USE THE PROSPECT'S PROBLEM OR DESIRE, ALONG WITH SOME NEW BENEFITS NOT YET SHARED, TO CRAFT YOUR CALL-BACK INTRO AND BUILD MOMENTUM.

Examples of a typical call-back:

"Hi,____. This is Mike Kaplan with XYZ Company. How are you? When we spoke yesterday, we were talking about the problem you had with _____ and also _____, and that it would be a big benefit to you if that could be solved, right?"

or,

"If you remember last time we talked, you mentioned to me that you wanted (desire), right? And you were interested in something that could _____"

It's always best to have one or two benefits that you hadn't yet discussed with the prospect to kick start your call-back and build momentum.

> *"After we hung up yesterday another thing popped into my mind that I wanted to mention to you ... (benefit)..."*

or,

> *"You know, since we spoke, I checked with my manager, and he mentioned one other thing to me I wanted to tell you ... (benefit)..."*

From there, the Closer builds momentum with a Yes-Pattern and closes.

Let's now look at example call-backs for each of the six reasons for a call-back.

CALL-BACK REASON #1

The prospect wants to see additional information on your product or service, such as a brochure, web site, fax, catalogue, sample, or demo.

Some sales situations necessitate that the prospect receive more information before he buys, and sometimes that information isn't immediately available. If the prospect asks to be sent more information too early in the sale (before your presentation), then treat it as an early brush off (see chapter 3).

Even when the request comes up late in the presentation, while still on the first call, the Closer should suspect that the request is a brush off and try to close the sale without sending the information.

Example:

Prospect: "Sounds good. Do you have any information you can send me (or leave with me) that I can look at?"

Closer: "Sure. I have a brochure I can send, but it is just the highlights of what we went over. Based on what you've heard so far, what questions or thoughts do you have?"

Prospect: "None, really."

Closer: "Ok, so based on what we just went over, what do you think of the product (service)?"

Prospect: "It sounds good."

Closer: "And you mentioned you wanted to solve _____, yes?"

Prospect: "Yes."

Closer: "And you can see how our (product/service) will be able to do that for you, right?"

Prospect: "Yes. Looks pretty good."

Closer: "Alright, then here's what we need to do... (close)."

If the prospect wouldn't close on the first call and insisted on getting information sent to him (which you should do, of course), here are some ways to start your call-back:

"Hi,____. This is Mike Kaplan with XYZ Company. We spoke yesterday regarding _____, and you wanted me to fax you our brochure, which I did. I also included some testimonials and a price sheet. The brochure I sent highlights many of the benefits we spoke about yesterday; however, I wanted to point out a couple more that will help solve (prospect's problem). First ..."

or,

"The brochure I sent highlights many of the benefits we spoke about yesterday; however, I wanted to review a couple of the most important ones that will help solve (prospect's problem). First ..."

Or, if you sent information and didn't get very far into the presentation on the first call:

"I just wanted to follow up on the conversation we had yesterday concerning the problems you were having with (<u>problem</u>). Why don't you grab the fax I sent? There are a couple of things I want to point out to you, ok?"

or,

"Now that you have the information I sent in front of you, I'm certain you can see it has all the benefits we talked about and more. It looks pretty good, doesn't it? And you can see how it would really help you with (<u>desire</u>), right?"

or,

"I wanted to get back with you. I assume you got the fax I sent. Did you look it over and see the benefits we talked about? Great, so you can see how this will be a big benefit to you (your family or your business), right?"

The Closer then builds a Yes-Pattern and closing opportunity.

If the prospect says he received the information, but hasn't read it yet:

"No problem, it'll only take a second, we can go over it together…"

or,

"That's fine. It's actually better that we spend a couple of minutes on it together—that way I can get you right to the most important features that will solve (<u>prospect's problem or desire</u>)."

If the prospect says he doesn't have the fax at hand:

"That's fine—go ahead and grab it, and I'll hold on!"

If you meet immediate resistance or a brush off on the call-back, push the hot button (problem or desire) that you found in the previous conversation to grab the prospect's attention.

Example:

Closer: "I know you're busy and I know you're time is valuable. That's why I sent the fax, and that's why I'm calling. You told me yesterday that you had (<u>problem</u>) and that you wanted to resolve it. So, if my product (or service) was able to solve (<u>problem</u>) and also (<u>benefit</u>), you'd want the facts before deciding whether to get it or pass it up, right?"

Prospect: "Yes."

Closer: "Great, so let's just take a few minutes and to see if what I've got can do those things for you, ok?"

It's possible that the prospect has already decided, before your call-back, to buy your product or service. You can assume this and design your call-back intro to go for the close.

Example:

"I wanted to get back to you regarding the (<u>product</u>) designed to handle (<u>problem</u>) for you. If you're ready, I'll go over the details on how to get this to you."

If the prospect is ready to order, proceed with the close. If not, this call-back intro will at least flush out the objection that you can handle to create an opportunity to close.

Sometimes the prospect will be very interested on the first contact, yet on the follow up call will be noticeably cold. There is most likely some other influence, such as someone he spoke to, that has turned him off. Look for and find the influence, because something certainly happened since your first call.

Example:

"Bill, I just don't get it. Just yesterday you were strongly interested on this. Did someone talk to you about it?"

or,

"I don't understand the sudden change of heart. Did you run into something that turned you off? Did you discuss this with someone since we last spoke?"

CALL-BACK REASON #2:

The prospect needs to get approval from a spouse or boss.

While still on the first call (or visit), the Closer should confirm that the prospect is fully closed on wanting the product before she goes to get approval from his boss, partner, or spouse.

"So, based upon what you're telling me, if this were your decision alone, you'd go ahead with this today, right?"

or,

"Putting the boss aside for a moment, what do you think of the products?"

If the prospect is not 100% sold himself, it's doubtful that he will be able to convince someone else. He may tell you, when you call back, that the boss said no when, in fact, he may not have checked with him at all.

Additionally, the Closer should always "train" the prospect on how to best sell his boss and get the approval.

Closer: "Just slipping a flyer on your boss's desk might not get him to sign off on this. The best thing would be to meet with him and go over it, wouldn't you agree?"

Prospect: "Yes."

Closer: "In order to ensure he gets this for you, he's going to need to see the overall benefit, right?"

Prospect: "Yes."

Closer: "Do you have a pen handy? Great, here are a couple of reasons why your boss will want to get the (<u>product or service</u>). You *should take notes, ok?"*

The Closer then lists out for the prospect the biggest reasons to buy (benefits) he can use to sell his boss, partner, or spouse on the purchase. The list includes the reasons that will benefit the boss and his business, as well as his employee.

Closer: "Ok, do you get the idea on how to go over this with your boss? Are you pumped up on this enough to where you think you'll get him to go with you on this?"

Prospect: "Yes."

Closer: "Great, what time today did you have in mind to get with your boss to wrap this up?"

The Closer should always try to first convince the prospect to allow him to speak directly with the boss or spouse, as she knows that she's best equipped with the information, skills, and determination to get the close.

Closer: "Will your boss sign off on your recommendation, or are you going to need to sell him on this?"

Prospect: "I will need to sell him on it."

Closer: "I know you're sold on wanting this. But, in order to ensure the best chance that your boss will sign off on this, he's going to have to see the benefits that are important to him and that's something you should let me present to him, and I can answer the questions he no doubt will have. Can we set up a conference call (or meeting) to do this?"

If you can't sell the boss, partner, or spouse directly, then make sure the prospect is 100% sold and well prepared to convince the person on his own. Have a set time to call back to see how it went.

The follow up call-back introduction is simple:

"I'm following up on our call from yesterday. I know you were get-

ting with your boss to sign off on getting (<u>product or service</u>*) and I wanted to check to ensure you were able to do that and go over what we need to do next."*

CALL-BACK REASON #3:

The call is interrupted and can't be completed.

There is an infinite variety of reasons why the first call or visit might have had to end unexpectedly. You can use that reason on the call-back to reorient the prospect and continue from there to build momentum.

If the interruption happened at the introduction or qualifying step:

"We spoke briefly yesterday. We didn't really have much time as you had a meeting to run to. As I mentioned the reason for my call is (repeat the first call intro)."

If the interruption happened in the middle of the presentation:

"We spoke yesterday about our (<u>product/service</u>*). You had to run into a meeting, and I just wanted to quickly finish what we were talking about. I had mentioned how our (*<u>product/service</u>*) will help you with _____, which you said was something you would be interested in resolving, right?"*

You would then continue the presentation and build momentum.

CALL-BACK REASON #4:

The prospect has never bought and hasn't been called in a while.

There are several call-back introductions that could work for this. This is just one.

Closer: "Hi _____, this is Mike Kaplan from ABC Company. We spoke a few times about getting you something that would help you *(solve problem), do you recall? Well, I wanted to ask: If we were able to get you something that could (<u>solve problem</u>), and I made you an offer you couldn't refuse, would you be interested?"*

Prospect: "Yes."

Closer: "Before I make the offer, I wanted to find out, do you still have a need to (<u>solve problem</u>)?"

CALL-BACK REASON #5:

The prospect became a customer at some time in the past, and is a prospect for buying again.

"Hello _____, this is Mike Kaplan from ABC Company. How are you today? Good. You purchased some of our (<u>products or services</u>) in the past, and I wanted to give you a call and let you know about some new products we just released. I'd like to take a second to tell you about them, would that be ok?"

Assuming you know the customer is satisfied, you can start off by asking how he is enjoying the product or service that he bought earlier. Get him to tell you several positive things, and then move into asking some questions to see if he has any other needs or problems that any of your products or services could solve.

You can even call previous customers to do a customer satisfaction survey. The questions should not only find out why they bought and the benefits they've enjoyed, but should also uncover any current problems or desires that another product or service of yours could solve.

CALL-BACK REASON #6:

The Closer can't close the prospect on that call or visit for whatever reason, and another attempt is needed.

The notes kept on previous calls are important here as you need to know exactly why the prospect didn't close. Based on that information and the prospect's hot problems and desires, the Closer will plan out her next call.

After a sales call, when a prospect fails to close, Closers often instantly realize where they erred in the call or what else they should've done. Sometimes even skilled Closers get caught up in the heat of the moment and make mistakes. The handling is simple: Note down what happened and, without the pressure of being on a call, come up with the next-call strategy.

There were many times where I ended a call unsuccessfully and then thought "I should've done this, or said that." In those cases, I simply called right back and continued the sale.

Example:

"Hi _____, It's Mike Kaplan again. I realized once we hung up that I forgot to tell you (or ask you) _____."

Or, if much later:

"After we spoke last I was thinking what you told me about your main concern, and I came up with a solution that I think you're going to really like..."

Be sure to have a strategy figured out before a call-back—don't try to wing it. Think solutions. Consult with an associate or manager to get ideas as needed.

EXERCISES:

Write your answers on a separate piece of paper.

1. What is a call-back?

2. What are the six circumstances in which a call-back would be necessary?

3. What is a "trial close," and when would you use it?

4. Practice, with a friend or co-worker, doing a trial close. Practice this until you can do it smoothly and confidently.

5. What notes should a Closer make on her first call or visit, and why?

6. What is the objective of the call-back introduction?

7. How is the call-back introduction's objective achieved?

8. Why is it best to hold back one or two benefits of your product or service from your first call (or visit)?

9. Practice, with a friend or co-worker, doing a 'typical' call-back. Practice this until you can do it smoothly and confidently.

10. Practice, with a friend or co-worker, call-back introductions for each of the six different call-back circumstances. Practice this until you can do each one smoothly and confidently.

14

LEADS

IF THERE WAS STEP BEFORE THE INTRODUCTION on the 8-Step Road Map, it would be Leads.

A "lead" is (minimally) a name of a prospect or potential buyer along with contact information. Leads are the raw materials that a salesperson must have; otherwise, there is no one to sell his product or service to.

Leads are generated from various sources, such as:

- Advertising – TV, radio, print, internet, direct mail, outdoor, etc.

- Customer database – Current and former buyers.

- Cold calling – Telemarketers calling to find prospects.

- Compiled lists – Yellow Pages, directories, subscription lists, past prospects.

- Referrals and word of mouth

- Trade shows and other gatherings.

Not all leads have the same value. The value is determined by how qualified the prospect is, how interested she is in the product or service, and how recent or "fresh" the lead is.

The most valuable leads are prospects who contact you because they are ready to purchase. Just below that in value are qualified prospects who contact you in response to an advertisement in order to learn more. Below that are qualified prospects who fill in a form on a website or send in a coupon from a direct mail piece to request more information, followed by a compiled list of prospects that have never heard of your product or service, but who are qualified to use it. At the bottom of this ranking is simply a list of names of people with phone numbers and no other information regarding their qualification. There are other types of leads that fit into various spots on this ladder, but these are the major distinctions to keep in mind.

Generally speaking, the higher the quality the lead and the greater the prospect's interest, the more it costs to generate. For instance, a company would have to spend a large amount of money on advertising and marketing to try to provide only qualified prospects that, from viewing the advertisement alone, called in and were ready to buy.

While the highest quality leads are terrific, there are usually not enough of them to go around or, if there are plenty, management likely doesn't need to pay high salaries or commissions to their salespeople as they don't need to be very skilled to take orders.

In my first sales position, selling direct mail advertising, the company I worked for did no marketing or advertising to generate sales leads. I had to hunt for qualified leads by digging through various magazines and direct mail pieces to see where likely prospects were already advertising.

If they were advertising elsewhere, they were more than likely qualified to also use my direct mail service. I would cold call them without any expectation that they would be interested in my call. I always appreciated it if they were receptive and interested, but once I had mastered the 8-Step Road Map, I knew that I would be able to skillfully build up their interest. Most important to me was quickly determining if they were qualified to use and pay for my service.

When I started my software sales company, I only had money to buy a compiled list (Yellow Page listings) of PC technicians and their business phone numbers.

My better salespeople did well with these lower quality leads as they were at least calling qualified prospects that had a need for our type of products and, since they were in business, had the money to buy. The prospects had zero interest in our company prior to being contacted, and in many cases, had little interest in our products at first. They were cold called, and interest was ultimately created using the 8-Step Road Map.

As you can imagine, these leads were tough to work for the salespeople who hadn't yet mastered the 8-Step Road Map. Some would complain that the reason they couldn't make sales was because "the leads are no good." It was true; the leads were no good if you were, at best, a Presenter, or worse, an Order Taker. The Closers who had mastered and used the 8-Step Road Map never complained about the leads. They just closed sales.

There is a lesson here: While it is easy to blame your lack of success on someone or something else, it doesn't mean that it's true, and that response is never the path to improvement. Before you blame leads for your lack of performance, look around, and if even one salesperson is closing sales with the same leads and you're not, maybe it's not the leads after all.

A CLOSER IS SKILLED AT CLOSING ANY KIND OF LEAD, REGARDLESS OF THE PROSPECT'S INITIAL INTEREST. AS LONG AS THE PROSPECT IS QUALIFIED, THE CLOSER KNOWS HE CAN AND WILL BUILD INTEREST USING THE ROAD MAP.

Obviously, if a company has the resources to invest in marketing and advertising to generate better quality leads (meaning qualified prospects who call, write in, or visit the company), it should pay off with a higher closing percentage and more sales. Marketing generates product awareness and interest, which a Closer then converts into sales.

As my software sales business grew, I reinvested profits into marketing and advertising to support the sales efforts. I generated better quality leads through print advertising, direct mail, trade shows, and the Internet. As a result, almost every salesperson markedly increased their number of sales. The people who knew and used the 8-Step Road Map, increased their closing percentages far beyond those who didn't.

I distributed the best (and most expensive) leads as rewards based on the previous week's sales production. If a company is making an expensive investment in lead generation, it wants to make sure that its investment isn't wasted. All the sales staff had an equal opportunity to earn the better leads—all they had to do was work hard and put up good numbers. By learning the 8-Step Road Map, they were able to accomplish this.

Running my sales company taught me another crucial lesson: The quality of leads, plus the level of hard work, plus the level of closing skill, equals the number of sales. While the company's management controls the leads, you, the Closer, can control your skill and how hard you work. So, even without the expensive leads of prospects that are already interested, a Closer can still increase his sales by increasing his hard work and skill.

(Leads x A) + (Hard Work x B) + (Skill x C) = # of Sales

A = the level of quality

B = the level of hard work

C = the level of skill

HOW TO MANAGE YOUR LEADS

One of the factors that affect the quality of a lead is the age of the lead (its freshness). Good marketing and advertising generates interest, which results in prospects taking the initiative to make contact with the company.

A Closer knows that the person's interest could be temporary and makes every effort to respond to that lead as fast as possible. He also knows the prospect may be looking at his competitors, which is another reason to move fast.

When he gets these types of leads, the Closer doesn't let them sit on his desk. In running my business, if I ever saw a salesperson not jumping on those expensive leads, I assumed that he already had too many leads and prospects to handle and would give them to another salesperson.

The original value of a lead is judged differently once the prospect is contacted and brought through the Step 2, Qualify. A very expensive lead may turn out to not be qualified due to the prospect not being able to actually use the product/service or pay for it. This is why a Closer would rather have a definite qualified lead with no initial interest than a very "hot" lead who called in from an advertisement but is in fact broke.

When I was selling direct mail advertising, it usually took two calls to close because the prospect needed to see a sample of our products, which I would mail with a complete pack of information. Today, with the accessibility of the Internet, prospects can usually be directed to a website during the first call to get the information they need, which allows for one-call closes in some situations.

Whenever I didn't close a sale after the first contact, I would assign the prospect a quality rating based on what happened in the call. I used a simple scale of "cold" to "hot." The more interested the prospect was and the greater her need and ability to pay, the better (or "hotter") I considered her. This rating can be noted either on the physical lead itself or tagged in your contact management software. You can also use a number rating system or something similar. After each subsequent call with a prospect, I would update her rating and note any change.

Why do you want to do this? So you can prioritize your prospects and manage your time with them accordingly. Not all prospects are equal, and if you don't have a system to quickly distinguish the hot from the warm or cold, you will not be managing your time for optimum efficiency and will be losing sales. "Hot" prospects aren't all made equally, either—some are hotter than others—and this can be tracked by adding a star or stars to indicate how hot they are. Again, use whatever system works best for you.

Now, just because you labeled the prospect "hot," it doesn't mean that it's a sure thing to close. For me, I found that I would need a certain number of hot prospects in my pipeline (in the process of being worked) to end up with one close. This way I knew what I had to do to get a close. If my closes were down, I would work hard to fill up my pipeline.

Also, just because you labeled a prospect warm or cold doesn't mean that she will never close, or that she should be ignored. It's your job to turn the cold into warm and the warm into hot. It's also your responsibility to use your judgment to decide how much time and effort you should invest in doing this. A Closer is always managing himself and his leads in order to work as efficiently as possible and close as many sales as he can in the time he has.

Every time a Closer closes a prospect that he's been working on, it frees up his time to work on other prospects. The longer he spends on each prospect without closing, the less time he has for finding the next hot prospect.

There's a trap that salespeople fall into where they're calling the same prospects over and over without closing deals, and they leave themselves no time to develop new prospects. They feel like they have so much time and energy invested that they can never give certain prospects up. It's like playing a slot machine—the more times you play without winning, the more you have to continue to get back the money you invested. When a salesperson just grinds away at prospects with no results, his morale and motivation drops, which only compounds the problem. After having failed to close a prospect despite many calls, the salesperson develops a negative or defeatist attitude. He "knows" that the next time he contacts that prospect, she will be resistive and will "probably come up with another way to get rid of him."

What has happened in many of these cases is that the salesperson gave up control to that prospect earlier, lost his confidence, and is now reluctant to be aggressive and take control back. He may be afraid that, if he suddenly gets more aggressive, he'll offend the prospect or even possibly lose her for good. The irony is he already lost her.

What to do?

Either get rid of all the overcalled, beaten-to-death prospects all at once and start fresh, calling different leads or start replacing one prospect at a time.

I always kept brief notes after each call that didn't close to refresh my memory and set a strategy prior to the next call. If I noticed that I had too many calls with a prospect, I would note down, "One more shot." If the prospect didn't close on the next call, I would never call her again and would get rid of the lead.

Knowing that I was going to toss the lead no matter what, if the prospect didn't close, I was relaxed and felt like I had nothing to lose. On the next call, my approach was more aggressive, confident and spirited. I wanted the close but wasn't desperate for it. This attitude allowed me to be in control of the sale and be a true Closer.

I closed countless "one more shot" prospects over the years. I tossed a fair share away as well. Whether I closed deals or tossed the leads, I unstuck myself from the tar pit that is a pipeline full of prospects who won't close, and my sales would always rebound.

Some salespeople may feel that leads are so scarce and valuable that they could never get rid of any of them. Ironically, it's that attitude that is hanging up their sales.

An alternative to throwing away overcalled prospects is to trade them with another associate. He takes yours, and you take his. To you, his old leads are new and you have no preconceived ideas about the people, or that you shouldn't be too aggressive. You won't feel stuck to his "one more shots" like you do with yours, and the same goes for him.

HOW MANY LEADS?

The ideal amount of leads for a salesperson is an amount that keeps him busy all day, but not so many that he feels unable to fully work with each person. With too many leads, a salesperson might also be unwilling to put in the time and effort to push through their prospect's objections and give up on the ones that show resistance.

If he has too few leads, he will likely spend too much time on prospects that aren't going to close and fall into the trap mentioned earlier.

BALANCE OF PROSPECTING AND CLOSING

Part of managing your leads involves making sure that you keep a proper balance of finding new prospects along with closing existing ones.

If you concentrate only on prospecting without putting enough time into closing the people you have in the pipeline, your sales will suffer.

If you focus only on closing your existing prospects without finding new ones, your sales will peak then crash as you will run out of hot prospects to close.

Avoid the cycle of feast and famine by keeping a proper balance. Even if you build up a large enough base of customers who can be continuously resold, you still need to find time to get new customers, if only for insurance purposes.

HAVE THE NEXT DAY SET UP

At the end of each day, before going home, I always set up my list of prospects to call for the next day, which were broken into categories: very hot, hot, warm, cold, and raw. This way, I was ready to go the moment the day started. I would typically call a couple of colder prospects first thing to warm up and get into the zone.

REFERRALS

A great way to maximize the amount of hot leads is to ask for referrals (names of prospects) from your new customers after each close (after you have the method of payment). When you call a referral, you want to include in your introduction that your customer asked that you call.

"Hi, _____. This is Mike Kaplan with ABC Company. Joe Smith asked me to call you regarding _____."

It takes discipline to remember to ask for referrals, but it often pays off in free, high quality leads. A referral usually wants to know what her friend or associate just bought, and the fact that she knows someone personally who owns your product or service lends to its credibility.

If the customer is in a rush at the end of a close, or you forgot to ask for a referral, you can always call back later and ask.

Even though customers are the ideal source for referrals, you can also ask prospects for them as well. If you don't ask, you won't get.

There are many books with great techniques on how to ask for and get referrals. A simple approach that I often used went like this:

"One last thing, as a favor, can you tell me a few names of people you know who you think could benefit from my product/service?..."

"Can I get their phone numbers from you too?..."

"Would you mind, when I call them, that I tell them that you asked me to give them a call?"

If you can, ask the prospect to tell you what each one does and what she thinks would be important to mention to them.

If your customer is reluctant to refer you people that are her direct competitors, you can say something like this:

"Excluding your direct competitors, who else do you know that you think could benefit from our products?"

ADD-ON SALES

To maximize your revenue per prospect, add products or services on to the sale after the prospect closes on the primary product or service. See "Add-on Sales" in Chapter 10: How to Close.

SUMMARY

There is an art to the management of your leads (and time), and getting skilled at it will greatly affect the amount of sales you can make daily.

Use what you've learned in this chapter to create a system that works for you, and figure out how to get the most sales in the shortest time possible.

EXERCISES:

Write your answers on a separate piece of paper.

1. What is a lead?

2. What factors determine the quality of a lead?

3. What is the first lesson to know when it comes to leads?

4. Why should new leads be contacted as soon as possible?

5. Why do you want a system to rate the quality of your prospects?

6. Work out a system that you will use to rate the quality of your prospects. What is it and how do you define each category?

7. Other than the sale itself, what additional benefit does a Closer get from closing his prospects as quickly as possible?

8. What trap can a salesperson fall into if he thinks there's scarcity of leads?

9. What should a salesperson do if he finds himself in the trap of calling the same leads over and over with no sales?

10. What is the ideal number of leads for a salesperson?

11. Why should a Closer keep a balance of looking for new prospects and closing existing prospects?

12. Why do you want to ask for referrals from your customers after the close?

13. Practice, with a friend or co-worker, asking for referrals after the close. Practice this until you can do it smoothly and confidently.

14. Practice, with a friend or co-worker, the introduction when calling a referral. Practice this until you can do it smoothly and confidently.

15

THE CLOSER PERSONALITY

BY READING THIS BOOK THOROUGHLY AND mastering all of the exercises, you will be light years ahead of those who do not know or use all of the steps of the 8-Step Road Map. But, there is another huge factor in determining how successful you can become.

I can train ten salespeople on every principle and technique in this book and have them do all the exercises until they each equally know what to do, but they will not end up closing the same amount of sales even with the exact same product.

Why is that?

A large part of their success depends on their willingness and ability to assume the personality (character traits) of a Closer.

Every profession requires a person to assume a set of qualities and character traits particular to that profession. For instance, some of the personality traits of a successful firefighter would include courage, dedication, self-sacrifice, caring, and desire to help. Imagine a firefighter who lacked courage or a desire to help others. How successful could he really be, even if he knows how to put out fires?

Some people are born with the personality and character traits that are suited to the sales profession. Many inherently have a good number of these ideal traits, but not all, while others have very few.

Some people believe that you either "have it" or you don't when it comes to a sales personality. Luckily, that's not true.

WHAT MATTERS IS WHETHER A PERSON HAS THE WILL-INGNESS AND ABILITY TO LEARN AND ASSUME THE CHAR-ACTER TRAITS OF A CLOSER.

We all have our own day-to-day personalities that our friends and relatives know (and hopefully love), but that personality might not be enough, or even appropriate, to become a Master Closer. Perhaps you only need to adjust (or add) one or two things, or maybe you need a major overhaul.

To some degree, it's like being an actor who takes on the identity of a character. Like the actor, you need to be "in character" when you are performing your job.

There are several characteristics that comprise being a Closer. The ones below are most universal and make up the essence of a Closer.

PERSONALITY TRAITS OF A CLOSER

1. Conviction—Closers fully believe in the product or service they are selling. They know it is valuable and will help their prospects; they wouldn't sell it otherwise. They know what their product or service is capable of and what its limitations are.

2. Honesty—Closers <u>never</u> lie to or deceive a prospect. They don't make false claims or exaggerate the features and benefits of their product or service. If their product or service is good, is priced fairly, and they know how to sell, why would they have to lie? They don't make promises that they or the company cannot keep just to get a sale. Prospects rely on the Closer's honesty.

3. Control—Closers know that sales don't just happen on their own. They know that they must be willing and able to positively control their prospect's attention through the 8-Step Road Map and ultimately persuade them to buy. They push through any apprehension or fear they may have when it comes to controlling or directing others.

4. Interested—Closers always express a sincere and strong interest in their prospects. From the things they say to how they act, Closers make the prospect feel that they are there to help them and be of service. Closers are not only driven by paychecks and money, but are also motivated by their desire to help others.

5. Energetic—Closers approach their profession with lots of energy. They mentally prepare themselves for the start of each day. They know the job of sales can be demanding, so they keep themselves in good mental and physical shape. They make sure they muster up the energy and enthusiasm needed before each call or visit. They never give a dull performance, nor allow themselves to go on automatic and sound uninspired.

6. Positive outlook—Closers know the value of having and acting in a positive manner and understand how that influences prospects to buy. They avoid people who are negative, recognizing them as sources of distraction and possible failure. They are confident with an attitude of, "I want the sale, but I don't have to have it," which keeps them from becoming desperate and too careful out of fear of losing the sale.

7. Problem Solver—Closers are solution-oriented. Their minds are tuned to rapidly think of creative, helpful solutions. They are confident that every problem or barrier they encounter can and will be solved. Whatever the problem the prospect offers up, the Closer knows, one way or another, it can and will be resolved to the benefit of everyone involved.

8. Persistent—Closers have a dogged determination to close each sale. They know that objections and other barriers are part of the game of sales and that, to win, they need to persist long enough until they persuade the prospect to buy. Not only are Closers persistent during a sale; they are also persistent and work through any setbacks they may encounter in their career. They know persistence can often compensate for any lack of skill or know-how.

9. Hardworking—Closers know that in order to achieve the greatest success possible, they must be willing to work hard. They have the drive and desire to succeed. They are rarely idle or distracted from their work. They are willing to make the necessary sacrifices and put in the extra time to get the job done.

10. Goal-oriented—Closers have defined daily, weekly, and long-term goals that they use to propel themselves to success. These include sales and income goals as well as other personal, family, and career objectives. They have a burning desire to succeed and reach those goals.

11. Focused—Closers arrange their lives in such a way so as to not get distracted during the period of time that is devoted to work. They do not get side-tracked by others in their pursuit of their goals.

12. High Standards—Closers have high standards when it comes to the quality of their work. The way they dress, carry themselves, accomplish their tasks, and represent their company are of the highest professional standards.

13. Initiative—Closers take their own initiative instead of waiting for someone else to direct them. They need very little, if any, management. They respond well to the positive input of others, but don't need someone else to motivate them. They arrive early to be sure they are set up and ready to start on time, and they'll stay late, if needed, in order to accomplish their objectives and targets.

14. Knowledgeable—Closers realize that the more they know about the profession of selling, the more productive and successful they will be. They spend time reading sales and motivational books, observing other salespeople's successful actions, and seeking ways to improve and streamline what they are doing while being careful not to neglect or change what has been proven successful. They stay up-to-date on all the features and benefits of their product or service, and they know how to use them in order to get sales. They are always willing to learn more product knowledge as long as it has relevance to being able to close more sales.

15. Team Player—Closers recognize that they are part of a team and that their success, to a large degree, depends on the effectiveness of the overall company. Closers are aware that there would be no sales job if it wasn't for the dedication and hard work of the management and administrative members of the team. They understand and appreciate what the other team members contribute to their success. Closers also know that the success of the other salespeople on the team is important to the longevity and success of the company.

16. Responsible—Closers know that they are responsible for their own success. When they fail, they do not seek to blame the prospects, the leads, the economy, the product, other staff, or management. They keep statistical records of their sales and revenue and use that information to judge their performance. They also take responsibility for their customers, ensuring they are satisfied with the product or service and taking steps personally (or getting others) to correct any problems as they arise.

I'm sure you have many of the above traits, to some degree, already. I suggest you rank yourself from one to ten, with ten being the strongest, on how strong you are on each trait. Note your strengths and weakness. Work on developing as many of the above traits into tens as you can, and be the Closer.

EXERCISES:

Write your answers on a separate piece of paper.

Rank yourself, one to ten with ten being the strongest, on how strong you are on each personality trait of a Closer. Write what you can do to improve each of the above traits that are less than a ten.

1. Conviction

2. Honesty

3. Control

4. Interested

5. Energetic

6. Positive Outlook

7. Problem Solver

8. Persistent

9. Hardworking

10. Goal-oriented

11. Focused

12. High Standards

13. Initiative

14. Knowledgeable

15. Team Player

16. Responsible

16

WHEN YOU NEED HELP

THERE ARE MANY TIMES IN EVERY SALESPERSON'S career when things do not go according to plan. From a momentary drop in sales to serious slumps, all salespeople, at least occasionally, run into trouble.

What separates a sales professional from an amateur is how they respond to and navigate through these difficulties.

Closers don't typically concern themselves very much with short-term declines as they know they are more or less a normal part of selling. However, when sales drop significantly for an extended period of time, they know the change didn't happen on its own. They know something caused it—most likely something they did, directly or indirectly. And, they know they need to do something about it if they want it to improve. They avoid blaming others or playing the victim, and they discipline themselves from rationalizing their poor performance on things outside their control, such as the economy, leads, products, company, or management. Even when it is determined that these things are a problem, the Closer focuses on what he did or didn't do to allow them to ultimately affect him.

There are two rules of thumb that have served me well whenever it came to debugging my own sales performance or that of my sales-people.

While it may seem obvious, the first rule is to look for and find what the actual cause of the problem is. A simple application of cause and effect will often uncover the source of the sales trouble. Whenever I was able to locate the correct cause and then fix it, sales would always improve. If not, I knew I either didn't find the correct cause, or if I did, that the right actions were not taken to resolve it.

Occasionally, the cause may be someone other than you, or something out of your direct control, but most often it will be something that you did that you shouldn't have, or something that you stopped doing that you should have continued. In other words, you have changed something in what you were doing prior to your decline in sales. That change, if located and addressed, will fix the problem.

To do this, start by narrowing down when a change was likely to have occurred. Closers do this by keeping statistical records of their sales performance. I always kept a weekly sales graph when I was selling, and so did the salespeople who I managed. By looking at the chart, you will be able to immediately spot when the decline started. You then focus on the period of time just prior to the drop in sales and search for what changed in what you were doing.

The change could be anything that negatively affected your ability to close sales: dropping or altering a step on the 8-Step Road Map, how you manage your leads, the number of calls or visits you make, your attitude, something from outside the office that affected you personally, and so on. Whatever it is, it will make sense once you spot it. Sometimes you have to dig just a bit earlier, or beyond, the first answer to find the real underlying cause.

You can do this on your own, or if needed, have a sales manager do this with you to help locate the cause.

When I noticed that the sales on a salesperson's chart had declined significantly during the last few weeks, I would direct his or her attention back to just prior to the drop, their last good week of sales, and ask one or more of the following:

"Did you change anything in that period of time?"

"Did you start doing anything differently around that time period?"

"Did you add anything new, or drop anything out that you were doing?"

"Did anything happen around that time or earlier that affected you in some way?"

The cause isn't necessarily what you are experiencing now. It's easy to say, "Well, it's my attitude. I just don't have confidence," or, "I don't have the drive or energy to do this." These attitudes are definitely affecting performance now, but are really symptoms of something having occurred or changed *earlier*. This is particularly true if your attitude hasn't been able to improve just by noticing it.

There are many possible causes. Here are some that I have found with salespeople on a regular basis:

- They partially or completely dropped the Qualifying step of the 8-Step Road Map and ended up wasting time on unqualified prospects.

- They stopped looking for new prospects and spent all their time trying to close what was in their pipeline. They failed to keep a proper balance of prospecting and closing so as to ensure that there would always be a pipeline full of future closes.

- They decided, after landing a large account, or seeing another salesperson do so, that they would only spend time on big accounts and forgo all others, even though their prior success was built on closing small-to medium-sized accounts.

- They became less energetic or aggressive at the close. Earlier they had failed to close a prospect who complained that they were too pushy. In response, the salesperson decided that he needed to be less demanding and thus became less persistent and would give up after the first objection or two.

- They decided, for whatever reason, that they didn't need to work hard but had to work *smart*. They became lazy, and their number of calls, contacts, and presentations dropped significantly, which resulted in their drop in sales.

- They started jumping right into their presentation without first uncovering the prospect's problem or desire or setting up the presentation per the 8-Step Road Map. As a result, they could no longer generate enough interest in their product to get a close.

- Someone said negative things to them about working in sales, and they came into work unsure and lacking the burning desire to succeed.

- Someone in the office said negative things about them, the company, management, or the product, and it has distracted them.

- They had some sort of upset or problem with management.

- They started partying and staying out late, and they began coming to work tired.

- They changed the way they were managing the use of their leads or time.

- They received a customer complaint and became unsure about their product being as good as it really was.

- They decided to use e-mail more often to try to get closes, while using fewer in-person calls or visits.

- They forgot or never really knew what the purpose of the presentation was, changing it from being a tool to create closing opportunities to something less effective.

- They no longer acted on buying signals when they occurred, and they bypassed opportunities to close.

- They dropped out one or more of the personality traits of a Closer that were vital to their success.

These were just some of the common ones. There are many more, but whatever it is, if the correct reason can be identified, it will make sense to the salesperson and will become something they can fix.

A sharp Closer will be vigilant to prevent these changes in procedure or attitude from ever starting, but if they do, she will at least be alert to them early on and can correct them before they take their toll on her attitude and confidence. The longer it continues without handling it, the deeper the attitude and sales drop.

If you cannot quickly find the cause from the questions above, then look over the 8-Step Road Map and the personality traits of a Closer, along with other information from this book, and use them as a checklist for possible changes.

If that doesn't quickly help you spot the cause, then tape record one or more of your sales (if you sell on the phone) to use to critique what you are doing. If you sell prospects out in the field, or otherwise cannot record the sale, then have your manager sit in on a few sales visits with you. You want to compare how sales should ideally be done, per this book, and how you are actually doing them. You can do this on your own, or have your sales manager do it with you. The recording will reveal which actions or personality traits you might have changed or what you are doing differently. Note: Be sure to follow all state and federal laws regarding recording sales calls.

Once you locate what you were doing wrong, take the necessary steps to fix it. Find the appropriate exercise(s) from this book that will help you to do this. If your sales begin to bounce back, then you know you found the correct cause and resolved it.

Whenever this first rule didn't work and I wasn't able to easily find the reason why sales were down, then my second rule was to stop looking for the reason and to just focus on *working* my way out of the slump.

Because my attitude and confidence had usually taken a hit from failing to close sales for too long, I needed a win to revitalize my spirits. I decided to stop worrying about closing prospects, instead focusing on either doing customer relation calls or calling on raw leads to find qualified prospects to add to my pipeline. These were both things I was certain I could do.

These customer relation calls simply involved calling on customers to see how they were doing with my product (or service) and if there was anything they needed. No pressure, just good public relations. I purposefully stayed away from trying to close them.

With the pressure off of me, several things happened when I did this. I immediately felt better, and my attitude improved. I felt like I could again accomplish something related to my job. I was making my customers feel cared for, and I was adding valuable, new qualified prospects to my pipeline. Without fail, within a day or two of doing this, a prospect, out of the blue, would ask to buy. It was magic. All the anxiety of not closing was gone, my confidence was back, and the closes began to flow.

WHEN SALES DROP, EITHER QUICKLY FIND WHAT CHANGED JUST PRIOR TO THE DROP AND FIX IT, OR DECIDE TO WORK THROUGH IT. TEMPORARILY STOP TRYING TO CLOSE, FOCUSING INSTEAD ON PROSPECTING OR CUSTOMER RELATION CALLS, UNTIL YOU REGAIN YOUR CONFIDENCE.

In addition to charting the number of sales or revenue, I would also keep a daily record of the number of calls, contacts, and presentations I made. Knowing that a certain amount of each one resulted in a sale, I could manage myself accordingly. If I wanted more sales, I increased the number of daily calls or contacts. You can have all the skill of a great Closer, but if you don't make enough calls or visits, your numbers will suffer.

Keeping a weekly chart of your sales will also serve as a reminder of how good you really are (particularly when you hit a slump) and that the current difficulty is only temporary.

Finally, in order to protect yourself from slumps occurring in the future, I recommend that, throughout your sales career, you spend some time every week investing in your sales knowledge and skill. This can include reviewing this book as well as other sales and motivational books or lectures. Observe, as often as you can, what the top Closers in your company are doing that makes them successful. All of this feeds your success and helps you be a better Closer.

EXERCISES:

Write your answers on a separate piece of paper.

1. What are the two methods of debugging yourself when you find you're in a sales slump?

2. How can you protect yourself from sales slumps in the future?

17

THE FINAL WORD

YOU HAVE TRAVELED THE WHOLE 8-STEP ROAD MAP and now understand the fundamental steps of selling, from Introduction to Closing, and know how to use them. While there is much more to learn about sales, you now know the basic essentials that apply to every sale.

Because you know the underlying purpose and objective of each step of the 8-Step Road Map, you can adjust or modify them as needed to fit your particular product/service and business. You can come up with your own wordings and techniques (and test them) in order to achieve the purpose of each step. You can study other techniques and the "tricks of the trade" out there and properly evaluate them to determine if and when they would be useful.

However, just knowing these principles and techniques is not enough. You need to know them cold. You need to practice each step of the 8-Step Road Map until you know the entire sales progression 100%. You need to use what you've read in this book daily until it becomes second nature.

If you haven't already done so, I urge you to go back and complete all of the exercises at the end of each chapter. Practice them with a co-worker or friend until you can do each smoothly and confidently. Once you master a step, move on to the next and begin practicing.

Once you have mastered all of the steps individually, you are ready for the final test.

FINAL EXERCISE:

Practice, with a friend or co-worker, the entire 8-Step Road Map from beginning to end selling your product or service including handling various objections. Practice this until you can do it smoothly and confidently no matter what objections are thrown your way.

CONGRATULATIONS!

You now know the 8-Step Road Map. Use it every day to make unlimited sales and be a Master Closer. I wish you great success!

BONUS REPORT

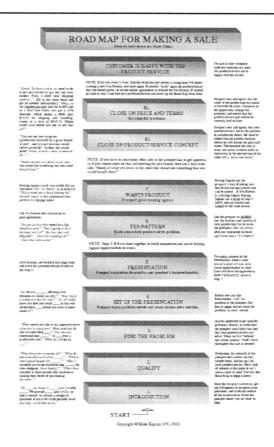

How would you like to have at your fingertips a single-page chart summarizing everything from this book?

Having read the book, you've learned and hopefully practiced everything you need to know to be a master closer. To ensure the best results, I've designed a chart to aid you in your day-to-day selling.

This free chart includes:

- Each of the 8-Steps to making a sale.

- The underlying principle and purpose of each step.

- Suggested scripts for each step.

Now that you know what to do, there is only one step left to guarantee your success: use what you know daily to create an abundance of sales!

Download this free chart today and close anyone, anytime, anywhere!

Visit www.bitly.com/roadmap-report now to get this free bonus report!

WOULD YOU DO ME A FAVOR?

Thank you for buying my book. I'm positive that if you just follow what I've written, you will be on your way to being the best salesperson that you can be.

I have a small favor to ask. Would you mind taking a minute to write a blurb on Amazon about this book? I check all my reviews and love to get feedback (that's the real pay for my work—knowing that I'm helping people).

Also, if you have any friends or family that might enjoy this book, spread the love and tell them about it!

If you have questions or run into some difficulties, or if you'd just like to tell me what you think about my book, shoot me an email at msk2131@gmail.com. I'd love to hear from you.

Thanks again, and I wish you the best!

Mike

WANT MORE?

Try my on-line sales course
Secrets of a Master Closer
for free!*

Being able to close sales nearly at will requires a complete system of training that ensures you actually *master* and *use* the necessary skills.

We have created what we feel is the most effective sales training system available that ensures a student not only understands what he or she learns, but more importantly, can effectively apply the sales skills resulting in the maximum amount of success.

We have all the components necessary to guarantee that you or your sales team become Master Closers.

*Go to **www.secretsofamastercloser.com** and do the first 2 lessons at no charge.

> " This course delivers an 8-Step program for closing sales. It is one of the best courses on selling I've ever done and I will use this information for years to come. Closing is the key to sales and this course provides everything you need to be successful. "
>
> – G. Tu

" Secrets of a Master Closer is the best training that I have ever done. I have been in sales for well over 10 years, and this course helped me tremendously. I wish I had done it 10 years ago. Make this the next training you do. It is really good and worth every penny! "

– C. Lloyd Jr.

" I am a sales manager and I learned priceless information from the Secrets of a Master Closer course. We now have all our sales reps doing this on-line training and following Mike Kaplan's 8-Step road map for success in being a master closer. I highly recommend Secrets of a Master Closer to any sales manager or trainer to use to train their entire sales team. "

– Tammy J.

" Secrets of a Master Closer is a great on-line course for learning how to close sales. I can tell you that it gets results. Just three lessons into the course, I had my personal highest ever sales in my company! "

– C. Bernot

" This is by far the best course ever on closing and the sales process. If you want to excel in closing then do this course. "

– M. Muzamil

" Other sales books I've read and seminars I've attended are inspirational and tell you what the problem is, but don't seem to address it directly. So far I feel I've learned more in the first 2 lessons of your on-line course than anything else I've done. "

– C. Lindsay

Made in the USA
San Bernardino, CA
09 November 2015